A SEARCH FOR WISDOM AND SPIRIT:
THOMAS MERTON'S THEOLOGY OF THE SELF

A Search for Wisdom and Spirit

THOMAS MERTON'S THEOLOGY OF THE SELF

Anne E. Carr

University of Notre Dame Press
Notre Dame, Indiana

An excerpt from Thomas Merton's poem "Hagia
Sophia" from *The Collected Poems of Thomas Merton*
is used by permission of the publisher, New Directions Publishing Corp. Copyright © 1962 by The
Abbey of Gethsemani Inc.

Paperback edition 1989
ISBN 0-268-01735-2

Library of Congress Cataloging-in-Publication Data

Carr, Anne E.
    A search for wisdom and spirit.

    Bibliography: p.
    Includes index.
    1. Merton, Thomas, 1915–1968—Contribu-
tions in theology of the self. 2. Man (Christian
theology)—History of doctrines—20th century.
3. Self—History—20th century. I. Title.
BT701.2.C2955 1987   233'.092'4   87–40352
ISBN 0–268–01727–1

Manufactured in the United States of America

CONTENTS

FOREWORD by Brother Patrick Hart   vii

ACKNOWLEDGMENTS   xi

INTRODUCTION   1

1. SEEDS OF THE SELF   10

2. SEEKING THE SPIRIT: THE CHRISTIAN INHERITANCE   34

3. CONJECTURES AT A TURNING POINT   54

4. THE WISDOM OF THE SELF: LEARNING FROM THE EAST   75

5. "I LIVE NOW NOT I . . . "   96

6. THE STORY OF THE SELF   121

EPILOGUE   141

NOTES   149

SELECTED BIBLIOGRAPHY OF BOOKS BY THOMAS MERTON   165

INDEX   167

FOREWORD

As the twentieth anniversary of Thomas Merton's death is commemorated, we are once again confronted with the mystery of this monk whose life and work continue to have considerable impact on both religious and secular society. How does one account for this phenomenon? Certainly Merton was a person of his time, who articulated the deepest yearnings of the human spirit, and constantly addressed the most vexing problems that have ever confronted humanity. But the essential thing about his writings was the fact that his commentaries on the religious life of faith as well as the gravity of the world situation in which he lived arose from his own "inner experience." Like Karl Barth, who died on the same day as Thomas Merton (December 10, 1968), he balanced the Scriptures in one hand and the contemporary scene in the other, especially during the last years of his life as a monk and hermit at Gethsemani.

Although a number of biographies have appeared during the past two decades following his death, and innumerable studies (at least a hundred doctoral dissertations and magisterial theses are registered at the Merton Studies Center of Bellarmine College in Louisville), there is still a need for just this kind of book by Sister Anne Carr on Merton's theology of the self. It was a subject Merton returned to again and again during his twenty-seven years as a monk, always addressing the question with a language that reflected the spirit of the times, and adjusting his words to the needs of an ever-expanding audience.

What the present volume attempts to do, and I would add
successfully, is to point out the reasons for Merton's relevance
for our times. The author makes it clear that although Merton
was not a systematic theologian in the strict sense of the word,
he definitely was "a theologian of the monastic and mystical traditions." She is convinced that it is "precisely this other kind of
theology which is the source of Merton's attraction for so many."
And I would agree: Merton always wrote in such a personal way
that allowed his readers to identify with him and his struggles
and never-ending search for God. Yet, his explorations and reflections were not of the kind that catered to an introverted and
isolated individual's search. Rather, as the author brings out so
well, "his reflections on the self address some of the deepest needs
of contemporary Christians."

Thomas Merton is portrayed here as one who grew and developed into what the author calls "a new universality." It was born
of his involvement in the social concerns of the sixties, together
with his enormous and wide-ranging correspondence with other
artists and poets, thinkers and writers, or just ordinary persons
who found comfort in writing to and receiving a "word" from
this man of God. Then add to this his extensive readings in
Sufism, Hinduism and Buddhism (Tibetan in particular), which
led him to "a new breadth in his understanding of the religious
quest."

With much primary material still unavailable to the student
of Merton's work, I believe it will be some years before we have
a really satisfactory picture of this prophetic voice of our times.
There are still at least four volumes of Merton letters to be published, in addition to the personal journals and notebooks which
were restricted by Merton himself for some twenty-five years following his death. In view of this restriction of the primary
sources, it seems all the more remarkable to have this study
which focuses on the very heart of Merton's teaching. I enthusiastically recommend this book to all persons who are interested
in religious practice, whether Christian or non-Christian. The

message of Thomas Merton transcends all religious denomina-
tions and racial barriers, as this book makes abundantly clear.

Brother Patrick Hart
Abbey of Gethsemani
25 July 1987

ACKNOWLEDGMENTS

This little book has been a long time in the making. And there are many people to be thanked for their help and encouragement along the way. The book began as an over-long essay. And it was Walter Burghardt, S.J., of *Theological Studies,* who originally suggested that it be expanded and developed into a small book. Mary Jo Weaver, of Indiana University, read the original manuscript and made many careful suggestions, as did Rozanne Elder of Cistercian Publications. Lawrence Cunningham, of Florida State University, was a more than helpful reader whose comments developed into a genuine dialogue about some of the theological issues in Merton's thought and about Merton's continuing impact on American students. I thank all these for their help.

Special thanks go to Franklin I. Gamwell, Dean of the Divinity School of The University of Chicago, who has been generous in providing me the time to complete the research and writing. Ann Rice, of the University of Notre Dame Press, raised important questions about the overall shape of the book and encouraged me in the editorial process, as did Betty Prevender of Mundelein College, friend and constant editorial consultant. Elena Procario prepared the index with care and efficiency. And my religious congregation, the Sisters of Charity, B.V.M., have long provided an environment of love and support.

I would also like to add thanks to Brother Patrick Hart for his kind words in the Foreword. Although I have never met him, every student of Merton is indebted to him for his continuing and essential contribution to Merton studies.

I dedicate this book to the several groups of Merton students who have helped me to clarify his thought in countless ways and to the memory of Thomas Merton, who continues to live among us in his life and work.

INTRODUCTION

Why another book about Thomas Merton? So much has already been written about this man. There have been biographies about his cosmopolitan early life and his dramatic conversion, studies of his work and writing as a monk, analyses of Merton as social critic, essayist, and poet, and as explorer of the world's religious traditions. All these in addition to Merton's own numerous works. Someone has remarked that Merton's books and books about him represent something of a "cottage industry" in our culture as new generations of students, Christian or not, young and old, women and men, newly discover his writing and become "hooked." They are attracted, perhaps, by Merton's spiritual writing or by his autobiographical reflections or his poetry. The sustained, even devoted, interest of so many suggests that this fascination is not just a fad that soon will wear itself out.

But how explain the continuing and compelling attraction to a person who, as a young man, walked away from involvement with the ghetto and its poor, marginalized ones for the beauty and peace of a contemplative monastery in the country? Certainly most religious people today are well aware of the Third World, its poverty and dependence, and acutely conscious too of the "underside" of our own nation. They are repeatedly reminded of their call to collective political, social, and economic action to attend to the needs of the world and to express overtly what Latin American theologians and, more recently, the United States Catholic Bishops have named "the preferential option for the poor."

1

Then why, in particular, a study of Merton's thought about the self? We live in a time and place, especially as Americans, that has been criticized for its narcissism, self-concern, and individualism.[1] Concern with the self can seem simply out of place for Christians today. Prayer, meditation, and contemplation suggest an inward turn in which, for a time at least, one attends to God and to one's own relation to God in such a way as to become intensely conscious of one's self in trying to reach out to God. Such a concentration on self can seem to mean forgetting the real problems of the world, an escape into isolation or introversion. But this, I believe, only seems to be the case.

For, paradoxically, even as many today experience a new and heightened sense of social and political responsibility, a deep spiritual hunger pervades contemporary sensibilities as well. Many people have turned inward in search of an integrating center within the self that can unite committed work in the world with a deep and focused interior sense of self, incorporating not only relationship to the world and to others, but finally to God. The search of many, whether Christian or not, is for an integral way, a spirituality, sometimes called a mystical-political orientation that unites the concerns of both self and world. After several decades of rapid religious change and experimentation—and without denying the important contemporary conviction that love of neighbor *is* love of God—many are at the same time turning or returning to older forms of prayer, meditation, and contemplation in search of ancient wisdom about finding God and the authentic meaning of the self. The question of the self remains central even within the most socially conscious of Christian perceptions. Who am I? And where is God? Each of us, ineluctably, asks these questions in the struggle to shape our lives responsibly in the world.

Hence there may be value, precisely at this time, in a sustained and serious Christian theological reflection on the meaning of the self. For *self* is an ambiguous term. It can mean the center of highest personal and religious responsibility; it can equally suggest an egotistic concern for self-fulfillment—selfishness—

that is especially questionable in a time of pressing social concerns. The writings of Thomas Merton provide not simply the record of an individual search for God and for the self, an important and inherently interesting record for study and reflection, but they are a unique resource that has special symbo!:c and theological value for religious searchers today.

For few American Catholics of his time were as deeply conscious as Merton of social and political problems, or analyzed them with comparable insight and courage. Nevertheless, the question of the self as a fundamental spiritual issue remains a central, enduring theme is his writing, from the beginning to the end of his life. At several stages in his life journey, Merton dwelled at length on the meaning of the true self and the false self, the real and the illusory self, the inner and the exterior self, framing the issue somewhat differently in each context.[2] His successive reformulations indicate that the question was never completely answered for him. The problem of the self remained an intense concern for Merton, and he understood it as a central issue for religious thought and experience generally. In a very broad sense, he sketched the outlines of what may be called a symbolic theology of the self.

Over the last decade, as I have rediscovered Merton for myself and have found diverse groups of students eager to join me in studying his work, I have become convinced that Merton's thought represents more the dated reflections of a once-popular monk and spiritual writer. I have become convinced that Merton is a profound and powerful theologian in his own right. Not a systematic theologian in the usual sense, he is rather a monastic theologian whose works retrieve Christian traditions that may have been slighted, if not forgotten, in our contemporary understanding of theology as dialectical argument, rational clarity, and systematic thought. Theology includes these dimensions, of course, but it is not confined to these, as we are reminded by those who advocate the importance, indeed the primacy, of a narrative or metaphorical or symbolic theology.

Thus this study of Merton is undertaken in the conviction

that there *is* room for a study of his life-work as a theologian, a theologian of the monastic and mystical traditions. And it is undertaken in the conviction that it is precisely this other kind of theology which is the source of Merton's continuing freshness and attraction for so many. Moreover, his reflections on the self are not the sort of explorations that cater to an introverted and isolated individualism. Rather, they address some of the deepest needs of contemporary people who struggle to balance the demands of an increasingly complex life.

Merton made no claim, of course, to be a systematic theologian.[3] The issues he addressed were those he struggled with in his own life. Christianity, the religions of the world, religious experience, all these he wrote about from the perpsective of his own experience in faith and the ways of prayer, in deep personal engagement and often agonizing doubts about himself. He constantly questioned his writing, his *persona* as an author, his vocation as either a monk in a community ("cenobitic") setting or as a hermit. Finally he came to question even the traditional contemplative and mystical patterns of Christian spirituality in which he was trained and which he studied in depth. Though his analyses of religious and theological issues were not systematic, they were nevertheless serious, immensely learned, and continue to have profound influence on masses of readers.

One reason for the influence, the enduring significance, and the already classic status of Merton as a religious writer is surely that he lived through a turbulent period of ambiguity about the vitality of the old forms of interiority, prayer, and asceticism, as well as uncertainty about the Christian understanding of the self within the context of a rapidly changing religious culture. His struggles and his explorations of the fragmented self are very much ours, just as is ours his search for wholeness and the true self in a painfully divided world and a sometimes polarized church.

Clearly, Merton's experiential explorations, rooted in the Bible, the writings of the church and monastic fathers and of the mystics of the Christian, Islamic, and Buddhist traditions, represent a kind of theology. However, it is best described as an autobiographical theology in which his own texted life story has become an important symbol to religious seekers of many different traditions and some of no tradition at all. Merton's writings on the theme of the real and illusory selves, conjoining personal and theoretical reflections, are a significant example of his autobiographical theology.[4]

In this context it is important to note that Merton is always conscious of his craft as a writer, even in his personal journals and autobiographical sketches. He is always an artist, recreating reality in his words, including the "reality" of his own life. Thus he *selects* the events about which he writes, carefully chooses the words and metaphors by which he creates, and does this with a reading audience in mind, even in his apparently casual and anecdotal reflections. It is in this sense that Merton's life is a "work," a crafted text that can be read by others, despite the distance in time and space, and even sometimes in religious belief.

As a religious thinker, Merton found his home in an older theological tradition which might also be called the theology of mysticism—or, better, contemplation. In a retrieval of the early traditions of Eastern Christianity, he sought to explore a form of thought which did not separate the head from the heart, the thirst of the intellect from the drive of the spirit. "For the Greek Fathers," he wrote,

> "Mystical Theology" and "Contemplation" are two ways of saying the same thing. The term "contemplation" is borrowed from Greek philosophy. Both terms mean the hidden knowledge of God by experience. . . . To be precise, theology (*theologia*) refers to the highest contemplation of God, . . . the triune God. Contemplation (*theoria*) refers rather to the contemplation of God in creation, and in the action of Providence in the world.[5]

A theology of mysticism or contemplation, on Merton's terms, need not be conceived as something esoteric or extraordinary, but can be understood simply as the exploration of a fundamental experience of God, available to anyone. The traditions of mysticism and contemplation belong to all Christians and, if we believe Merton, they may have important insights to offer today, as more Christians turn to older forms of prayer.

Or, if we locate Merton within the Western context of the medieval distinction between *ratio* as discursive reasoning and *intellectus* as a higher understanding by connaturality (participation and experience), the heart of Merton's thought lies in the latter realm. Thus his writing speaks to the need, felt by so many today, to explore a personal realm of experience that includes but goes beyond the intellectual and is sometimes spoken of as the realm of imagination, intuition, or wholeness. For Merton's is a contemplative theology that seeks to be radically experiential. It is, as well, a symbolic theology in its immediate, metaphorical, and disclosive character. His religious writing functions through image and symbol rather than through logic and argument in suggesting more than it literally says, in connoting both the familiar and the unknown, both present experience and future possibility. It is a language that speaks to the heart as well as the head. And with the question of the self, Merton seizes upon an aspect of contemplative tradition that is a highly charged and evocative contemporary symbol.[6]

It is the ancient tradition of *theologia,* a "tradition of wisdom and spirit," that Merton espoused for himself and recovered for his readers in a contemporary context, even as he transformed its content, under the rubric of the self. He saw the contemplative tradition not only as the nourishment necessary for his own monastic and solitary vocation, but as a desperately needed antidote to the various poisons in contemporary Western life. Those poisons bear many names: fragmentation, dehumanization, an uncontrolled technology, the loss of nature and the natural world, the war machine and the bomb, violence, racism, materialism, physical and spiritual poverty. With these in mind he wrote,

I am more and more convinced that my job is to clarify something of the tradition that lives in me, and in which I live: the tradition of wisdom and spirit that is found not only in Western Christendom but in Orthodoxy, and also, at least analogously, in Asia and in Islam. [Our] sanity and balance and peace depend, I think, on keeping alive a continuous sense of what has been valid in [our] past.[7]

Merton's discussions of the real and illusory selves can be understood within the scope of the contemplative theology that he called the "tradition of wisdom and spirit," *theologia* in its ancient meaning. He brings this tradition to life precisely by showing how it continues to live in his own experience.

This study describes several texts in which Merton deals with the problem of the self and offers an interpretation of those texts in the light of their biographical and historical contexts. It does so not with any great hope of finally resolving Merton's ongoing question, but with the more modest aim of simply tracing and illuminating dimensions of the problem as he sees it at various stages of his life and of noting the rather startling changes of perspective which emerge at each stage. The expanding horizons within which Merton views the recurrent motif reflect, I believe, something of the changing spiritual quest of our times.[8]

For example, Merton's early work recalls, for those twentieth-century Christians formed in the patterns of a Reformation, Counter-Reformation, or nineteenth-century theology and spirituality, old patterns of religious understanding that are somewhat ambiguous today. They are ambiguous most of all because of the rhetorical extremes in which they advocate self-denial as well as denial of the goodness of the world and so seem to encourage profound self-doubt and mistrust of our experience of ourselves and of the world. Still, we recognize that there is important truth in the ancient patterns. Beneath these extremes of rhetoric and beneath the more recent historical overlay is a hidden truth for which we hunger as we affirm, in a new way in the post–Vatican II era, the goodness and grace of our world and of our selves. This is so even as we become more intensely aware of the capacity for evil and sin that lies within these same selves, as we look back at recent history and as we contemplate the possibility of nuclear or ecological disaster resulting from our own human actions.

Merton's explorations of the ancient traditions of wisdom, and the slow, subtle changes of interpretation he works on these traditions in the course of his own struggles and questions, enable us to recognize both the continuity and the change in our own spiritual selves as contemporary Christians. We know ourselves as truly Christian, faithful to the ancient wisdom and truth that is named in Jesus as the Christ and the movement he began, together with the long tradition that bears his name. And we know ourselves truly as people of this world in our newly emerging global awareness that we are members of a "world church" in a religiously pluralistic world. The experience and thought of the later Merton reflects that changed perception of both self and world within which our contemporary search moves.

The theme of the self occurs most clearly and explicitly in sustained fashion in Merton's writings in eight different texts, which can be grouped so that they represent different though overlapping biographical and historical situations in his life and thought. The texts are: *Seeds of Contemplation* (first published in 1949, and fully revised after several interim revisions as *New Seeds of Contemplation* in 1961); *The Silent Life* (1956); "The Inner Experience" (begun in 1959, with several later revisions, unpublished as a book but recently selected and edited as eight articles in *Cistercian Studies);*[9] *Conjectures of a Guilty Bystander* (1966); *Zen and the Birds of Appetite* (1968); and, finally, *Contemplation in a World of Action* and *Contemplative Prayer,* both published after Merton's untimely death, the first in 1969 and the latter in 1971. By limiting this study to just a few texts, rather than surveying all of his works, I hope to probe a single theme in some depth.

The twenty years spanned by the dates of these texts come

close to spanning Merton's life as a monk and religious writer. The changes rung on the theme of the self as one works through the writings chronologically demonstrate the intensification and transformation of the issue for Merton. From the young self-negating and world-denying monk of 1949 to the mature self-affirming and world-embracing Asian traveler and religious seeker of 1968, there is striking change as well as deep continuity in the search for the true self.

Examination of the texts themselves allows us to probe Merton's explicit reflections on different aspects of the question of the self, as a central and consistent theme in his work and as it reflects the changing circumstances of his experience of the world in which he lives and prays and searches for wholeness. The autobiographical and biographical contexts are provided first by Merton's other writings, especially his autobiographies and more personal journals and notebooks. While all of Merton's writing embodies his characteristic style of immediacy and personal engagement, they are nowhere better exemplified than in the journals and notebooks that are at the heart of Merton's autobiographical theology. These contexts are further opened to us by the writings about Merton of those who knew him well, especially Edward Rice's provocative sketch and the two recent biographies by Monica Furlong and Michael Mott.[10] This horizon helps to illuminate the personal struggles and concerns as well as historical developments which are the background of Merton's more theoretical discussions about the problem of the self in the texts.

1

SEEDS OF THE SELF

Seeds of Contemplation was written in 1947 in what Merton later described as the second period of his monastic life (1944–49), the time from his first vows until his ordination to the priesthood.[1] At the end of his novitiate, his health broke down and he was assigned to writing and translating while studying philosophy and theology in preparation for ordination. During this period he wrote *The Seven Storey Mountain* in 1945 and 1946 and *Waters of Siloe* in 1948. Between these two major pieces of autobiography and monastic history he wrote the first and most popular of his many spiritual works, *Seeds of Contemplation*. Merton's friend Edward Rice evokes the physical and spiritual climate of those years in *The Man in the Sycamore Tree*.[2]

The monks' lives at the Cistercian (or "Trappist") monastery of Gethsemani in Kentucky were rigorous and austere: they slept on straw and boards, shivered through the Kentucky winters in ill-heated buildings, and scratched at heat rash in heavy, infrequently changed medieval clothes in the summer. The food was spare and the manual labor heavy. Rice says that Merton tried not to worry about his health, "became very serious, pietistic, self-effacing [and] . . . accepted without question or qualm whatever his spiritual directors taught." It was in an experience of monastic euphoria, heightened by disgust with the "world" he had left, that Merton wrote *The Seven Storey Mountain*. A similar tone pervades the first edition of *Seeds of Contemplation.*

The message of the latter book is a simple one: the contemplative experience which is the heart of monastic life is meant not only for monks but for all Christians. Merton's conviction is that nothing in the book is revolutionary or even original; it is simply orthodox Catholic tradition. Besides the Gospel and the Rule of St. Benedict, he draws on the writings of the twelfth-century Cistercians, especially Bernard of Clairvaux, and the sixteenth-century Spanish Carmelite, John of the Cross. In an important way, however, the book *was* revolutionary at the time. Immensely popular, it seemed to come as a breath of fresh air to an American Catholicism pressed between a sentimental piety on the one side and a moralistic or rationalistic interpretation of dogma on the other.

Merton's recovery of the contemplative tradition for ordinary readers brought new meaning and spiritual depth to the authoritative faith and prescribed morality of Catholic life in the late 1940s. For he wrote vividly about the possibility of the *experience* of God in faith, the possibility of a spiritual adventure that was the *experience* of union with God through prayer. Apparently he was right in thinking that "since the interior life and contemplation are the things we most of all need," the book's reflections "ought to be something for which everybody . . . would have a great hunger in our time."[3]

The implicit theological framework of *Seeds of Contemplation,* in which Merton's first discussion of the real and illusory self is set, is one which maintains a clear dichotomy between the natural and the supernatural. The natural is in sharp contrast to the supernatural—it is as slavery to freedom, as natural desire to supernatural desire, as love of captivity to genuine liberty, as the hardened heart to Christian love. This context is, nevertheless, one of indirect but significant experience of God's providence. All created things—trees, food, cold, heat, birds, streams—are sacramental signs of God's care. But Merton writes that it is only the saint who is able to see these connections in things without making strained analogies. Only the saint, even without explicit reference to God, is capable of seeing, talking about, loving all things in God's will.[4]

In this context, Merton writes that "the only true joy on earth is escape from the prison of our own selfhood"; created things only bring pain and hurt. Their most insidious effect is to deaden one to the pain they inflict. Instead of worshipping God through creation, "we are always trying to worship ourselves with creatures," and this is "to worship nothing"; it is hell. Unlike other parts of creation, persons must be more than natural selves; they must be saints. Yet, paradoxically, sanctity means being oneself.

> It is true to say that for me sanctity consists in being myself and for you sanctity consists in being *your* self and that, in the last analysis, your sanctity will never be mine and mine will never be yours, except in the communism of charity and grace.[5]

Salvation itself involves "the problem of finding out who I am and of discovering my true self." The problem is complicated because of human freedom: one is left free by God to be what one wishes but only God really knows the secret of one's identity, "can make me who I am or rather . . . who I will be when I at last fully begin to be."[6]

The "seeds" of contemplation are in fact the seeds of one's own identity planted continually by God in the core of human liberty. They can be refused in a denial of one's own existence, one's very self. The possibility of refusal is rooted in original sin, or the "false self" with which every individual is born. Reflecting the classic Augustinian notion of evil as nonbeing, Merton writes in *Seeds of Contemplation*:

> I came into existence under a sign of contradiction, being someone that I was never intended to be and therefore a denial of what I am supposed to be. And thus I came into existence and non-existence at the same time because from the very start I was something I was not.[7]

The autobiographical flavor of this passage is striking when one recalls the opening words of *The Seven Storey Mountain*:

On the last day of January 1915, under the sign of the Water Bearer . . . I came into the world. Free by nature, in the image of God, I was nevertheless the prisoner of my own violence and my own selfishness, in the image of the world into which I was born. That world was the picture of Hell, full of men like myself, loving God and yet hating Him; born to love Him, living instead in fear and hopeless self-contradictory hungers.[8]

The stark reality of original sin, not as a dogma but as the *experience* of one who has undergone dramatic conversion, lies behind Merton's notion of the false self. In *Seeds of Contemplation* he describes himself as "the thing that was born of my mother" and comments that if he is still the same person, it were better that he had not been born at all. This false or illusory self, the self that "I want myself to be but who cannot exist because God does not know anything about him" is a spector that constantly shadows each individual. It is a "private self" which wants to exist on its own outside of God and is an illusion that is difficult to recognize. For "most of the people in the world there is no greater subjective reality than this false self of theirs."[9] Merton's harsh judgment on his own former self is extended to a similar judgment about the rest of humankind, at least his contemporaries outside the monastery.

Moreover, "all sin" begins in the assumption that this false self with its egocentric desires is the center of reality, the ordering pole of the individual's universe. Thus pleasures, experiences, power, knowledge, and even love, are accumulated to make one's self perceptible to the world and to oneself. But this self is a hollow, "objectified" person, doomed to a destruction which, when it occurs, will "tell me that I am a mistake."[10]

In sharp contrast to the illusory and sinful self is the secret self of one's real identity. This is an identity hidden in God, and because God's simplicity is indivisible, it is somehow even *identical* with God. Thus the only way to find oneself is to find God. This finding of the true self in God is "immensely difficult." For beyond the knowledge of God's existence and something of God's nature which is possible for human reason, the *discovery*

of God and of the true self is a matter of "contact" or "possession," an experiential knowledge which is impossible to achieve
on one's own. But there is a point, "a metaphorical apex of existence" in which one's contingent reality is suspended in being
by God and where God can be met in "real and experimental
contact." One does not find this point, however, but is found by
God.[11]

This theological perspective, which no doubt reflects Merton's
study of the seminary theology of the 1940s and 1950s, is the
traditional Christian view that maintains a clear and final distinction between the Creator and the creature, such that, in the terms
of Thomas Aquinas for example, while there is a real relation
between creatures and God, there is only a logical relation or
relation of reason between God and creation. This distinction—
much discussed today in relation to process thought, which holds
that there is a real internal relation between God and creatures—
intends to preserve the absolute freedom of God in relation to
creatures and the nonnecessity or gratuity of creation. Under the
rubric of grace and nature, the Catholic tradition, especially in
the Thomistic heritage, also proposes a second gratuity: the utter
gift of redemption and grace is such that, while there may even
be a natural desire on the part of human persons for grace and,
ultimately, the Beatific Vision, nevertheless there can be no human exigency or natural demand for grace. As a participation in
the divine life, and actualized in the theological virtues of faith,
hope, and love, grace is always utterly free, a gift.

The implication of these traditional distinctions between Creator and creature, and between grace and nature, for monastic
and mystical theology, heightened in an Augustinian or anti-
Pelagian perspective that insists that grace is unmerited, is that
the monk or ascetic, or any Christian, who seeks to realize the
presence of God experientially can only prepare or dispose the
self for this new experience of God. The experience itself remains
grace and gift. Grace goes before and enables human striving for
God. Grace is not the answer to the human search for God, but

the original, though hidden, impetus for the search itself: one would not seek God unless one had already in some sense been found by God.

Merton's distinctive notion of the false and the true self is itself derived from his own Cistercian tradition. In his history of monasticism, *The Waters of Siloe,* he attributes the notion of the "false self" to Bernard of Clairvaux. "In St. Bernard's language," Merton says, "our true personality has been concealed under the 'disguise' of a false self, the *ego* whom we tend to worship in place of God. The monastic ascesis is entirely directed against this *ego.*"[12]

Merton frames the cosmic Christian doctrines of creation and sin in terms of the individual problem of the false, illusory self in *Seeds of Contemplation;* the doctrine of redemption or grace which is the framework for the discovery of the true self is realized in contemplation. In line with the theological distinctions between Creator and creature, grace and nature outlined above, Merton is careful, in 1949, to distinguish Christian contemplation from any form of active or aggressive self-mastery. In contrast to his later deep appreciation of eastern religions, the young monk writes:

> If, like the mystics of the Orient, you succeed in emptying your mind of every thought and every desire, you may indeed withdraw into the center of yourself and concentrate everything within you upon the imaginary point where your life springs out of God: yet you will not find God.[13]

No "natural exercise" can conquer the utter transcendence of God or bring one to genuine contemplative knowledge. But God has already "come down from heaven" and has found each one, providing the superior reality of grace in which one can truly discover God. Christian contemplation is a participation in God's contemplation. "We become contemplatives when God discovers [God's] self in us; at that moment the point of contact opens out and the contemplative 'enters eternity.' "[14]

Merton founds the Christian contemplative experience in the doctrine of the supernatural missions of the triune God, as these are the foundation of the Christian life begun at baptism. For baptism introduces the Christian into the inner life of God, which is a life of trinitarian relationship.

> The Father, dwelling in the depths of all things and in my own depths, communicates to me His Word and His Spirit, and in these missions I am drawn into His own life and know God in His own love.[15]

In the self-communication of God which is begun at baptism, the discovery of personal identity occurs because God, who bears the secret of the personal self, begins to live in the individual not merely as Creator but as the "other and true self." Merton quotes Paul as he will often do in reflecting on the theme of the true self: *Vivo, iam non ego, vivit vero in me Christus.* ("I live, now not I, but Christ lives in me." Gal. 2:19–20.)

But, he points out, the baptismal communication of God's life, an ontological reality, takes on practical meaning and is realized experientially only through conscious human activity, through a series of choices that each of us is called to make between the false self of illusion, selfishness, natural appetite, even the "only natural" desires of virtue, and one's "true identity in the peace of God." Since the natural human mind and will are stubbornly impervious to the Word and Spirit, one must pray to be filled with consciousness of God and to be kept from sin: from lust and love of money, from vanity and covetousness, from envy and sloth. One must pray for and practice humility and love and especially *withdrawal*—withdrawal from illusion and pleasure, anxiety and desire, conflict and competition in order "to wait in peace and emptiness and oblivion of all things."[16]

Merton's perspective here reflects both a rich patristic sacramental theology of baptism and at the same time a rather depressingly negative spirituality in which natural human inclinations are viewed with almost total distrust. From a contemporary theological point of view which takes seriously the experience of grace, one might argue that his perspective is simply incoherent: on the one hand, the Christian is born by baptism into the very life of God, is interiorly transformed; on the other hand, this transformation seems to have no real effect on the experience of the one baptized. One is still inclined to the grossest kind of sin, still subject to that natural human mind and will which are closed, for all practical purposes, to the action of the divine Word and Spirit. Despite Merton's high theology of grace, in which God's action is paramount, the authentic living of baptismal life still seems dependent on human withdrawal from the ordinary world, which is filled with temptation and sin, and not with any genuine opportunity for deepening one's relation with God.

No doubt Merton's own autobiographical experience is at play here, as well as the negative, rigorous, and ascetic spirituality of De Rancé, the seventeenth-century Abbot of La Trappe, the French monastery which gave the name Trappist to Merton's own Cistercian Order of the Strict Observance. In *The Seven Storey Mountain,* Merton describes how his own life of dissipation and unhappiness had continued, even after his baptism, until he finally found peace at Gethsemani. And Gethsemani, in the 1940s and 1950s, followed the "French tradition" of La Trappe and kept its very strict rules.[17] It was, in fact, this rigorous tradition that attracted the young Merton as a symbol of giving *everything* to God in his own withdrawal from the world, a "world" that represented only corruption and distance from God. Yet even in this early book of spirituality, the first edition of *Seeds of Contemplation,* the gold of a more positive creational and sacramental theology, which was the fruit of Merton's study of patristic and medieval theology, can be discerned within the harsh spirituality of withdrawal that he advocates.

For this negative spirituality with its rather cold and suspicious interpretation of human nature is somewhat softened in later chapters of *Seeds of Contemplation* where Merton analyzes "integrity" as a similar problem for poets and religious people: the problem of being oneself. Again, the autobiographical overtones are clear. Merton was himself a gifted writer, the son of artist parents who were for him a family heritage of which he was always proud. As a boy, after his mother's death, he had lived in France and traveled with his painter father, Owen Merton. And Thomas Merton always maintained a deep respect for his father's work. Merton's own literary gift was not only a plaguing source of self-doubt and distraction in his early monastic life but it also represented an imperious internal demand of talent, a talent that found its outlet in an amazing literary productivity in these early years: poetry, several biographies of Cistercian saints (of which he will be quite critical in later times), and a number of studies of monastic life and contemplation.

Merton's aesthetic sensibilities were formed in the Scholastic tradition of Thomas Aquinas, particularly as interpreted by Jacques Maritain. He had made extensive use of Maritain's *Art and Scholasticism* in his master's thesis at Columbia University on the theme of nature and art in William Blake. In this study the important issue for Merton was the creative and intellectual character of art as a virtue resident in the *artist:* hence, slavish imitation of nature, for example, can never be real art; and technical facility, though necessary for a good work of art, is not sufficient. Art as a virtue entails primarily the intrinsic integrity of the artist before God.[18]

Thus, in *Seeds of Contemplation,* Merton compares the poet to the religious seeker and maintains that conformity to the usual or popular pattern means that one wastes one's life in the vain effort to be "some other poet, some other saint." Merton claims that there is an intense egoism, in fact, in following the crowd. Laziness and haste destroy both saints and artists who fail to be true to themselves. Complicating his own pattern, Merton writes that it takes heroic humility to be nobody but the self God intends.

You will be made to feel that your honesty is only pride. . . . You can never be sure whether you are being true to your true self or only building up a defense for the false personality that is a creature of your own appetite for esteem.[19]

In this difficult situation, his advice to his readers is that humility is learned from the struggle to keep one's balance: "continuing to be yourself without getting tough about it and without asserting your false self against the false selves of other people." Castigating those who try on systems like hats, he writes that one of the first signs of sanctity is that one seems crazy or proud, haunted by an ideal that only God understands. Human life never fits abstract norms of perfection, "what the books say."[20]

On the whole, however, the pattern in *Seeds of Contemplation* is consistent in its own norms. The illusion presented by the natural appetites is constant, and one's natural efforts to be one's real self are fruitless. They cut the individual off from other people by erecting barriers of contrast such that one ends up by admiring the distance between oneself and others. Even "saints" must contend with spiritual pride; this "worm in the heart" of all religious people deceives by the pleasure of self-satisfaction with one's virtue, which is claimed as a possession as one clothes one's private illusion of oneself with values that are of God. In what looks like humility, the "spiritual" person enjoys the admiration of others and secretly comes to despise them in a false competition; one takes oneself too seriously. For Merton, the only way around this problem of spiritual pride is to be content not to be a saint, to accept one's mediocrity and let God lead one in paths of darkness and confusion. Then one may come to see the reflection of God in others. "I must look for my identity, somehow, not only in God but in other [persons]. I will never be able to find myself if I isolate myself from the rest of [hu]mankind. . . . "[21]

Already in this early spirituality for ordinary Christians, Merton indicates his own personal attraction to the apophatic (unknowing) tradition of mysticism, the *via negativa* of, for example, the Spanish mystic and poet, St. John of the Cross. Merton brings the themes of obscurity, darkness, and confusion in the serious life of prayer to bear on the question of personal integrity. Acceptance of one's own mediocrity, that is, acceptance of one's fragmented and confused self as flawed, helpless, and vulnerable in relation to the peaceful love of others and especially love of God will finally, he affirms, bring one to that experience of love or simple acceptance of others. This question of love of other persons brings Merton to another favorite early theme as well, that of solitude. For love of others surely seems to imply giving thought to others, being with others, spending one's self and one's time with other people.

Yet solitude, the idea of being alone with God, meant something of central importance to the young Merton. The very idea of solitude had drawn him to Gethsemani where he had in fact discovered that the common or "cenobitical" life entailed a busy daily schedule of liturgical activity, living, working, eating, and sleeping in very close quarters with others. (The monastery's dormitories, for example, allowed only a very small space partitioned for each monk.) Even the writing to which Merton was assigned was done in the few hours he was allowed each day in the crowded "scriptorium" or novitiate library. He had very little real privacy, despite the monastery's strict rule of silence.

When Merton addresses the question of solitude in *Seeds of Contemplation,* he could very well have been talking to himself, for he writes that there is always a danger that one may seek solitude simply to escape from people one dislikes. But the only real basis for deliberate solitude for the Christian is the knowledge that it will help one to love God and others as well. For "love is my true identity. Selflessness is my true self. Love is my true character. Love is my name," Merton's words sing. The goal of solitude, and the contemplation to which it is ordered, is not a "heaven of separate individuals in which each enjoys a private vision of God but the common and shared contemplation of all in the mystical person of Christ." The earthly realization of this union with others remains obscure, known only in the darkness of faith, for "the more we are alone with God the more we are united with one another." But, Merton warns, it is better not to remember individuals in contemplation, since that would "tend to withdraw us from God and therefore from spiritual union with them. We remain more truly with them when we no longer know them." This is part of the "darkness" of contemplation.[22]

Merton is drawing here on the ecclesiological theme of the church as the Mystical Body of Christ, which had been the subject of a major encyclical of Pius XII in 1943. But in *Seeds of Contemplation,* his use of this conception of the unity of Christians in the one body of Christ reads like abstract dogma, with little or none of the experiential immediacy that is characteristic of Merton's best spiritual writing. This doctrine, with its powerful and concrete implications for Christian life in community and, one would think, for a monastic life founded on the Rule of St. Benedict, is simply asserted by Merton. It can be known or realized only in the unknowing or *darkness* of faith, he believes at this stage. Despite the long hours of liturgical prayer in common, hours spent in the singing of the hours of the Divine Office through the day and in the night at Gethsemani, and daily work in common with the other monks, Merton finds that other people are really a distraction from God and from contemplation. It is better that we "no longer know them." There is, for the Merton of 1949, no genuine sense of real Christian community and its goodness or its importance in the life of faith. And there is certainly no sense that community can be an aid to or a genuine expression of one's relation to God.

Once again the autobiographical overtones are clear. Merton had long struggled with the problem of relationships to others, even during his childhood. The problem was one of loving and being loved in a way that nevertheless enabled genuine freedom. In *The Seven Storey Mountain* he had written about a family with whom he had lived as a boy.

> As a child, and since then too, I have always tended to resist any kind of possessive affection on the part of any other human being—there has always been this profound instinct to keep clear, to keep

free. And only with truly supernatural people have I ever felt really
at my ease. . . . That was why I was glad of the love the Privats
showed me, and was ready to love them in return. It did not burn
you, it did not hold you, it did not try to imprison you in demon-
strations, or trap your feet in the snares of its interest.[23]

In 1949, Merton touched on the same theme in his journal, *The
Sign of Jonas*. He uses the image of transcending his own past
identities in order to be free for God:

> To belong to God I have to belong to myself. I have to be alone—at
> least interiorly alone. This means the constant renewal of a decision.
> I cannot belong to people. None of me belongs to anybody but
> God. Absolute loneliness of the imagination, the memory, the will.
> My love for everybody is equal, neutral and clean. No exclusiveness.
> Simple and free as the sky because I love everybody and am pos-
> sessed by nobody, not held, not bound. In order to be not remem-
> bered or even wanted I have to be a person that nobody knows.
> They can have Thomas Merton. He's dead. Father Louis—he's half
> dead too. . . . I shall not even reflect on who I am and I shall not
> say my identity is nobody's business because that implies a trucu-
> lence I don't intend. . . . Now my whole life is this—to keep un-
> encumbered.[24]

It has been said that Merton was seeking a kind of "non-
identity" that was in fact a religious self-transcendence.[25] This
non-identity was intimately connected with his own dilemma as
a contemplative monk and solitary, and as a social being and a
writer. It is as though he mistrusted and feared other people as
a danger to contemplative solitude and single-hearted love of
God. At the same time Merton was aware of the dangers of cut-
ting oneself off from others, of simply avoiding people one dislikes, of using solitude for selfish reasons, of a failure to love.

Merton's desire for solitude and his conviction of the necessity
of solitude for the life of contemplation are deep and instinctive.
This is apparent in *Seeds of Contemplation*. "Physical solitude, exterior silence, and real recollection are all morally necessary for

anyone who wants to lead a contemplative life," he writes. And although he maintains that the truest solitude is not something external, nor a place to which one can travel, but is a silence in the center of the soul, nevertheless some literal and physical isolation—"a room, some corner"—is necessary for setting oneself free, for "loosing all the fine strings and strands of tension" that bind one to the presence of other persons. Nevertheless, Merton remains self-critical about this hunger for solitude; "it is dangerous to go into solitude merely because you happen to like to be alone."[26]

It seems clear that the contours of Merton's personal quest for identity, or a loss of self in non-identity, his particular struggles as a monk and as a writer, deeply influence his analysis of the religious problem of the self at this time. In *Seeds of Contemplation,* he maintains that "in the love of Christ and in contemplation . . . we find ourselves and one another as we truly are," and so "become real."[27] But, he says, this finding of the self and others is a matter of no little difficulty. It is, rather, an anguish of balance-keeping between integrity and conformity, between humility and spiritual pride, between the real and the illusory self. It is also an anguish that Merton does not hesitate to name, for his ordinary Christian readers, as leading to the "night of the senses" and the life of infused contemplation wherein, as the tradition (especially John of the Cross) teaches, contemplation is "learned from God." The context of this learning is "a desolation where there is no food and no shelter and no rest and no refreshment . . . for the desires of . . . nature," "a darkness and obscurity and helplessness" which allows "God to strip us of our false selves and make us into the new [persons] that we are really meant to be." This action of God is experienced simply as defeat and requires one to remain quiet "in the muteness of naked faith," a light which is darkness to the mind.[28]

Merton now speaks of a new kind of prayer which is "utterly simplified" and "clean of images." It brings a spiritual joy in which one's nature, emotions, and selfhood have no part. Yet he himself uses a powerful image to describe this higher stage of prayer: "the clean, intensely pure intoxication of a spirit liberated in God." And the renunciation involved in the way to contemplation brings from Merton such homely advice as "minding one's own business" and initiating a "strategy" or a "campaign" to fight one's obvious vices. This is so although he counsels that deep and unconscious bad habits resist all planned campaigns and it is better to leave these to the initiative of God working either directly in the self or indirectly through other persons or events. On this score, the attentive reader today hears Merton excoriating *himself* as he remarks, "It may well happen that the true test of your contemplative vocation may be your willingness to give up St. John of the Cross, for a time, in obedience to a director who does not understand him"; and "as soon as God gets you in one monastery you want to be in another," as indication of his personal struggles at Gethsemani and his attraction to the deeper solitude suggested by the literature he has been reading about the hermits of the Charterhouse or the Camaldolese solitaries. We can see these struggles and the plaguing question of the self as the context in which he saw himself as a spiritual writer or "teacher" of contemplation too:

> *Contemplata tradere* implies two distinct vocations: one to be a contemplative and still another to teach contemplation. . . . But then, as soon as you think of yourself as teaching contemplation to others you make another mistake. No one teaches contemplation except God Who gives it. The best you can do is write or say something that will serve as an occasion for someone else to realize what God wants of him.[29]

Even here, in his work as a spiritual writer and teacher, the shadow of the self, the suspicion of a phony piety and the question of authentic identity lurked for Merton.

In the final chapter of the first edition of *Seeds of Contemplation,* entitled "Pure Love," Merton describes the three beginnings of the prayer of contemplation. In the first and the best beginning, images, concepts, and words disappear. In the second, more usual beginning, one passes through a "desert of aridity," an "interior suffering" in which one gradually becomes aware of the presence of God. In the third, "the will rests in a deep, luminous and absorbing experience of Love." But in all three of these beginnings, one remains aware of oneself as on a threshold of something as yet indefinite: God is present but still hidden. Even when the experiential contact with God deepens, one remains far from God. Why? Because "there are always two of you." And as long as this sense of difference and distinction remains, the fullness of contemplation has not yet become known.

"The next step is not a step" but an experience in which, Merton writes, "all adjectives fall to pieces" and metaphor itself becomes impossible. Nevertheless he uses metaphor and abstract concepts to describe the experience. "It is freedom living and circulating in God, Who is Freedom. It is love loving in Love. It is the purity of God rejoicing in His own liberty." And, on the theme of the self, Merton insists that this experience of contemplation is not something that God pours out into a created subject so much as it is God's *identification* of a created life with God's own life in such a way that "there is nothing left of any significance but God living in God."[30]

Is this the annihilation of the self? Or is Merton, despite his caveat about metaphor, himself going to rhetorical extremes in his effort to evoke that which is beyond human comprehension? His struggle and, he implies, his readers' struggle with the self in the life of prayer suggests at least that his own attempt to "lose himself," as one of his interpreters aptly puts it, means that the goal of contemplation, the traditional high point of Christian realization of the life of grace as participation in the life of God, entails an experience of loss of self. It is an experience in which the person is, as Merton says at the very end of *Seeds of Contemplation*, "vindicated and delivered and fulfilled and destroyed." That self can no longer think of itself as "something separate, or as the subject of an experience." That self cannot even any longer be subject to pride or desire, because there is no longer a "contingent self to which anything can be attributed."

> Here is [one] who is dead and buried and gone and [whose] memory vanished from the world and . . . [who] no longer exists among the living who crawl about in time. . . .[31]

Only God's identity remains in love and knowledge and joy, Merton concludes. And one wonders: about the extremes of Merton's own self-hatred and his distrust of ordinary human life as created goodness, and about the wide appeal of this book of contemplative spirituality, companion to *The Seven Storey Mountain,* in post–World War II America. Merton's biographers remark that Merton's writing at this period, especially his famous autobiography, drew increasing numbers of young men to Gethsemani, particularly veterans of the war, but younger men as well. Many of them did not stay in the monastery. One wonders if this vision of self-annihilation in God was not only intoxicating in its attraction but too extreme for a really Christian, that is, incarnational, foundation of spirituality.

Nevertheless, in the first edition of *Seeds of Contemplation,* Merton had retrieved for modern readers some of the richness he had himself uncovered in his own studies of the writings of the church and monastic fathers, especially those of Eastern Christianity, and the contemplative traditions of the mystics, especially St. John of the Cross. With his characteristic enthusiasm, he communicated his discoveries of the riches of these traditions in the simple, clear, and direct language of his own experience: an experience of dramatic conversion from the self to God, from the "world" to the monastery, from what he perceived as a corrupt culture to Christ, and from the "unreal city" to the peace and tranquility of the countryside of Kentucky. These several contrasts provide a series of fertile analogies and metaphors for the contrast between the life of grace, expressed in contemplative prayer, and the distraction and fragmentation of ordinary life in the world. Ordinary life, according to the spirituality of *Seeds of Contemplation,* is redeemed only by participating as much as possible in the contemplative goals of monastic withdrawal. Merton implies, at this time, that Christians "in the world" can share in the riches of the contemplative life, but only by becoming, in effect, their true selves as monks in the world.

Merton's own assessment of *Seeds of Contemplation* was mixed. When it appeared in 1949, he wrote that it lacked "warmth and human affection," was "cold and cerebral," and revealed his own underlying pride and selfishness. Some passages were "at the same time excessively negative and subtle and obscure." Yet he was glad that it had been written.[32] In 1961, after several interim revisions, he completely reworked it, commenting that the book had first been written "in a kind of isolation," by one who had no experience in confronting the needs and problems of others. In the intervening years, he says, his own solitude had "been modified by contact with other solitudes," that is, by the problems of the young monks he was now directing, and the "loneliness of people outside any monastery, . . . of people outside the Church." We think, of course, of his many correspondents and friends.[33]

And indeed, a new tone pervades the 1961 revision, called *New Seeds of Contemplation.* The entire book is less absolute, elitist, severe. The theme of the false and true selves is retained, but it is clarified by Merton's more explicit adoption of the specific personalist theory of Jacques Maritain. Maritain was, in Merton's judgment, one of the most important contemporary interpreters of the thought of Thomas Aquinas. And Merton had already made extensive use of Maritain's work in his 1939 master's thesis on nature and art in William Blake. Aspects of Maritain's thought are already apparent in the first edition of *Seeds of Contemplation.*[34] But in the thorough revision that is *New Seeds,* Maritain's distinction between the individual and the person is strikingly present in Merton's discussions of the false and true selves.

Maritain's theory of the person is straightforward and clear. He holds that Pascal's idea that "the ego is hateful" is the correlative contrast to St. Thomas' statement that "the person is that which is noblest in the whole of nature." Maritain writes that "if the selfish ego is hateful, the creative self is that which is noblest and most generous of all."[35] He explains this apparent contradiction in the appraisal of the person by maintaining that the human being is a conjunction of two poles, matter and spirit. The *individual* represents the material pole, the *person* represents the spiritual pole. In the Thomistic scheme as Maritain describes it, the individuality of all things, including human beings, is based in matter, understood as prime matter or pure potentiality or receptivity, a potency that is "an avidity for being," for form or the soul which, with matter, comprises a substantial unity. Thus "the human soul constitutes, with the matter which it informs, a unique substance, both spiritual and fleshly." Soul and matter are the two co-principles of the one human being. And matter is the source of the differentiation or the individuality of every being, including the human. Maritain writes:

> One might say that in each of us, *individuality,* being in one that which excludes from one all that other men are, is the narrowness of being, and the "grasping for onself," which, in a body animated by spirit, derives from matter.[36]

Insofar as the human being is a *material* individuality, its unity is precarious and tends to slip back into multiplicity, dispersal, and decomposition. As individuals or material beings, Maritain holds, we are part of the physical universe and subject to its determinations.

But insofar as the human is *person* or spirit, it is not so subject. The spiritual soul is the principle of creative unity, independence, freedom, and especially of love. For when one loves, the object of love is the deep, metaphysical center of the other existent being, beneath or beyond all the particular qualities which nevertheless are integrally part of the other.

In Maritain's view, this center is in some way an inexhaustible source of existence, of goodness, and of action, capable not only of giving but of *giving itself*—and capable of receiving not only this or that gift from another, but of receiving another *self* as gift and giver.[37] The person possesses and disposes of itself in an independence that is relative to the transcendence of God, who is the sovereign personality and who, in the supereminence of intellection and love is absolutely independent of matter. Personality is thus rooted in spirit and is the dynamic source of unity and inner unification, the source of expression and communication with the other in creativity and dialogue. Personality is, for Maritain, the image of God in human beings.[38]

Individuality and personality are united in each human being, and both are good. But it is only in relation to personality that individuality possesses its goodness. What is bad is to let individuality rule in the composite human being, for the free actions of the human being are drawn either into a movement that tends toward God, as the source of spirit, or toward the movement into the dispersion that is the direction of materiality. Maritain writes:

> In the moral order, [one] must win . . . freedom and . . . personality. In other words, . . . action can follow either the slope of personality or the slope of individuality. If the development of the human being follows the direction of *material individuality*, [one] will be carried in the direction of the "hateful ego," whose law is to *snatch*, to absorb for oneself. In this case, personality . . . will tend to adulterate, to dissolve. If, on the contrary, the development follows the direction of *spiritual personality*, then it will be in the direction of the generous self of saints and heroes.[39]

This framework of Maritain's thought, studied closely by Merton during his graduate years, thus provides him with a clear, metaphysical contrast for his own distinction between the true and false selves, one of the central metaphors for his own experience of interior division. It also provides for Merton and for much of the Catholic teaching of the time, an ascetic framework. For as Maritain continues, "[One] will really be a person, insofar as the life of spirit and freedom will dominate in [one] that of passion and of the senses."[40] Maritain's application of this theory to educational, social, and political concerns can also be seen as the philosophical basis for Merton's own later reflections on the social issues of the 1960s: violence, racism, technology, consumerism, and peace. In *New Seeds of Contemplation,* however, on the question of the true and false selves and in the context of contemplation and spirituality, Merton simply adopts Maritain's language: the false self is the "individual," the true self is the "person."

And *New Seeds of Contemplation* is structurally different as well: two new chapters which introduce the revised central material, and a final chapter, "The General Dance," present an apologia for contemplation. As symbolized in creational terms, contemplation is not an esoteric teaching but is universally significant. Contemplative knowledge is a knowledge that can only be suggested by words; it is an "experience of the transcendent and inexpressible God," a "gift of awareness," "the realization of the belief of every Christian that 'It is now no longer I that live but Christ lives in me.' "[41]

But contemplation is not a function of the external self or superficial consciousness that can be observed by mere reflection or described psychologically. For neither the "superficial I," nor the "empirical self," nor one's "individuality" is the real self, the secret person who in Christ is united to God. The external self that works and thinks, observes and talks about itself, is finally only a mask or disguise of the hidden self.

Contemplation is precisely the awareness that this "I" is really "not I" and the awakening of the unknown "I" that is beyond observation and is incapable of commenting upon itself. It cannot even say "I" with the assurance and the impertinence of the other one, for its very nature is to be hidden, unnamed, unidentified in the society where men talk about themselves and about one another. In such a world the true "I" remains both inarticulate and invisible, because it has altogether too much to say—not one word of which is about itself.[42]

Merton uses Descartes's phrase, *cogito ergo sum* ("I think therefore I am"), to highlight the contrast he wishes to draw. The *cogito*, he says, expresses a being that is alienated from its spiritual depths and has reduced itself (and God) to a concept or to an object like other finite objects of thought. Here again Merton is drawing on Maritain, who interpreted Descartes as holding that the soul is a complete being in itself and the body (or extension) another complete thing. In contrast, Maritain argued that the spiritual soul, the spiritual person that Merton calls the true self, is secondary and derivative in relation to the transcendent God; it needs simply to prepare and dispose itself toward awareness of God's presence within itself. Thus Merton says that contemplation is an "intuitive awakening," "the existential grasp of reality as subjective, . . . myself in existential mystery." There is no deduction (no *cogito*, no *ergo*) but only "I am," not in a tough assertion of individuality but in the humble awareness of God's presence in the self. No calculated strategy can obtain this awareness. "It is not we who choose to awaken ourselves, but God who chooses to awaken us."[43]

And thus, Merton says, Christian contemplation is neither the special privilege of quiet, reflective, prayerful temperaments, nor of those who have a taste for liturgy, but is a possibility, indeed is the vocation for all Christians. It is not trance, nor is it ecstasy, not enthusiasm, nor the ability to read hearts. These experiences may in some way momentarily suspend ordinary consciousness and the control of the empirical self, but they are the activity of the emotions, the unconscious, the forces of "id," not the "deep self." They may accompany authentic religious experience, but they are not contemplation. Nor is contemplation an escape from conflict, anguish, doubt. Contemplation burns out complacency, prejudice, clichés, and even holy conceptions until one *"no longer knows what God is"* because God is not a "what" but a "who," "the 'Thou' before whom our inmost 'I' springs into awareness."[44]

Finally, in *New Seeds,* Merton holds that there is an authentic human autonomy that is an imitation of God's creative activity; it is good, and is the basis for a higher possibility of God-likeness in the human spirit. For both in creation and incarnation the transfiguring presence of God presents one with a choice between two identities: a "shadowy autonomy" and the "hidden, inner person" in Christ and the Spirit. In Maritain's terms, there are two possibilities within each person and one can *choose* either individuality or personality as the path or direction for one's life. Individuality means, in this framework, attending to one's self or the hateful ego; the path of personality means attending to others and to God. Yet even the shadowy activity of the external self is the object of God's mercy. The disguise that one wears may hide not only the inner self but God "wandering as a pilgrim and exile in His own creation." *New Seeds* concludes that "we are invited to forget ourselves on purpose, cast our awful solemnity to the winds and join in the general dance."[45]

Seeds of Contemplation and *New Seeds* both reveal the theme of the self in the stark terms of true and false. Merton's emphasis is on experience, especially in its contrasting aspects as natural and supernatural, which he casts as the experience of sin and grace. The natural is almost entirely negative, the false self which comes into existence in a state of separation from God; divided within, one is alienated from one's own truth and identity. This universal predicament is the source of all sin. One can recover one's true self only in "finding God," a discovery that involves the experience of divine contact and possession, but paradoxically a discovery that is only received as a gift but for which one must carefully dispose oneself. In Augustinian terms, Merton depicts the individual as the microcosm in which the great motifs of creation, sin, and redemption unfold. And the reality of redemptive grace is experienced by the Christian in the prayer that is contemplation. Contemplation draws one into the supernatural realm to active participation in God's eternity. And preparation for the gift of contemplation demands intense prayer and withdrawal from the ordinary desires, conflicts, and the relationships of everyday life in a single-minded focus on God.

In the first edition of *Seeds of Contemplation,* however, it is also apparent that Merton is self-critical about his own sharp distinctions. He tempers their severity in affirming the complexity and subtlety within this pattern. No spiritual system really fits any person, and fidelity to one's integrity may look like pride. One can never be sure that one is being faithful to one's true self, the secret self that only God comprehends. And finally, Merton is ambivalent about the place of other people in one's contemplation. Theoretically, he maintains the unity of all people in Christ, that love of others is part of one's love of God, and that solitude can be pursued for selfish reasons. Practically, he distrusts the distraction from God which attention to others entails and he judges that it is safer to forget others and to allow God's love to transform one's human loves. The 1961 revision, *New Seeds,* removes all suggestion that other people represent a danger to contemplative union with God. In a new framework and with a compassionate tone the book suggests the possibility of the good autonomy of the person as contrasted to the false autonomy of the individual. It places clearer emphasis on the hidden, real self which emerges in the "dark light" where God meets the self in simplicity and distinct identities disappear. *New Seeds* registers much of the development in Merton's thinking on the self that the next two texts we will examine record in detail.

2

SEEKING THE SPIRIT:
THE CHRISTIAN INHERITANCE

Merton's next treatments of the theme of the self occur in texts specifically associated with the monastery: *The Silent Life,* published in 1957, and "The Inner Experience," a partly published work begun in 1959.[1] The first text dates from the end of Merton's self-designated "third period" (1951–55), during which he was appointed Master of Scholastics, and the latter from the beginning of the fourth period, after he became Master of Choir Novices. Both offices involved extensive study in preparation for conferences and classes and were positions of great responsibility in the monastery. Later Merton noted that in the latter period he had overcome the need to apologize for the limitations of his earlier work, especially the "artificial public image" of himself created by *The Seven Storey Mountain.* "I have tried to learn in my writing a monastic lesson . . . : to let go of my idea of myself, to take myself with more than one grain of salt."[2]

Merton's personal struggle with his various identities continues to parallel his discussions of the self in his writing. Rice reports that Merton told a friend in 1949: "Say that Merton is dead and never existed, and is a fake. Bogus Trappist exposed. Golf trousers under the cowl. Merton wears a necktie."[3] And in the middle of 1951, he wrote in his journal:

> . . . I have become very different from what I used to be. The man who began this journal is dead, just as the man who finished *The*

34

Seven Storey Mountain when this journal began was also dead, and what is more the man who was the central figure in *The Seven Storey Mountain* was dead over and over. . . . I think I will have ended up by forgetting them. . . . [That book] is the work of a man I never even heard of. And this journal . . . the production of somebody to whom I have never had the dishonor of an introduction.[4]

Certainly the fame of his autobiographical self made Merton uncomfortable, and he tried not to take himself too seriously. But something deeper was involved. There was a deadly earnest attempt on Merton's part to transcend the successive selves that emerged in each literary and spiritual expression, to lose himself in a sort of "non-identity."

Merton's work of teaching and directing the numerous young monks now attracted to Gethsemani, many of them drawn by his own writing, especially *The Seven Storey Mountain,* drew him to an intensified study of the Bible, the writings of the monastic and church fathers, theology, spirituality, and mysticism. He kept to a demanding schedule of teaching and writing and had continual health problems. Rice says that there was also tension in the monastery because of legalistic enforcement of the Rule and Mott records the series of difficulties between Merton and the Abbot of Gethsemani, Dom James Fox. One of their conflicts was because Merton repeatedly wondered about a life of greater solitude for himself as a Carthusian hermit or in a hermitage at Gethsemani. This desire was seen by his superiors as a sign of his own psychological and spiritual instability. Throughout the fifties Merton argued that the Rule of St. Benedict allowed for the progression of some monks to the eremitical or hermit's life; in 1960 Merton was finally allowed to have a small house built on the monastery property where he could spend several hours each day in solitude.[5]

In *The Silent Life,* written in the mid-fifties, Merton relates the notion of the true and false selves to his discussion of the meaning and purpose of monastic life, a way of life that appears scandalously useless to an irreligious culture. Although about the monastic way of life, *The Silent Life,* he writes, should also be relevant for anyone who takes the life of prayer seriously. And Merton clearly thinks, at this period of this life, that the monastic way is the most perfect expression of the Christian life. The monk, he says, is one who has taken the first commandment seriously, who devotes his entire life to seeking God, and who searches beyond dry abstractions for the direct experience of God attested by the Bible. Merton finds this understanding of the direct experience of God confirmed by his own reading of the mystical tradition, especially John of the Cross, his favorite mentor.

The monk, Merton writes, leaves behind "the fictions and illusions of a merely human spirituality to plunge himself in the faith of Christ." That faith is a light which "illumines him in mystery," a "power which seizes upon the inner depths of his soul to deliver him to the action of the devine Spirit." The monk's objective is the *liberty* that belongs to the inner life of every Christian and growth toward the *maturity* of the Christian faith. In choosing "the horizon of the desert" that is "the monastic church of the wilderness" over the "city of Babylon," one engages in a mysterious confrontation, a battle that will be waged in one's own heart.[6] The contrasting images of the city and the desert, in this early period, like the world and the monastery, the natural and the supernatural, and later, the scientific and the contemplative attitudes, are Merton favorites. The wilderness is linked as well to the image of the recovery of paradise through contemplation.

Under the rubric "Purity of Heart" Merton writes that the monk searches for God who is both everywhere and nowhere. If God is nowhere and is found by the monk, then it is impossible that the monk should remain the same "I." And if God is everywhere, then in some way God will be the monk's "own self." In entering this mystery of transcendence and immanence, one attempts in faith the complete gift of self, an "abandonment of oneself" to find union with God. Thus one strives "to be hidden, to be nowhere, to be no one." All the asceticism of the monastic life is ordered toward disposing oneself for this union with God. If ascetic practices are misused as ends in themselves they only "fill the monk with himself."[7]

The asceticism of the monastery centers on the virtues of humility and obedience. *Humility* serves to detach the individual from absorption in the self, gradually tearing down the illusory projections that have been erected between the individual and reality. The heart of the battle is the saving "despair" in which humility finally conquers one's attempt to be one's own god and in this despair there emerges the victory of "the real over the unreal." This conquest of self-preoccupation occurs only in the love of God and love of others in God: only love can accomplish "the complete forgetfulness of ourselves." The monk's flight from the world means "to leave oneself . . . and begin to live for others." And while the details of a monk's life may be changed, the central obligation to obedience is enduring and essential. For *obedience* serves to detach one from the stubborn insistence on living "as a self-assertive and self-seeking individual." One renounces one's deepest illusions about oneself. When these illusions die, the false self disappears and the light of God can appear in the humble place that is "empty of self." The monastic fathers, Merton says, termed this "purity of heart," a theme he refers to again and again in his writing on the interior life and the true self.[8]

Here Merton focuses on traditional patristic Christian themes —obedience and purity of heart—as central in his interpretation of the monastic life. Why does he choose these particular themes? No doubt because they are important in the tradition, but we may also conjecture about their personal importance for Merton. His experience in leading his own life and directing his own affairs as a young man in England had led to a wayward existence that brought him trouble, unhappiness, and even misery. The recent biographies that have brought to light Merton's irresponsibility in fathering a child while he was a student at

Cambridge suggest that, after his conversion, the strict demands of monastic obedience appeared to him as centrally important in leading one to the beginnings of bodily "purity" as the first prerequisite for an interior purity of heart that is a far deeper ideal for him, the point of obedience.[9]

Citing Cassian, Merton says that purity of heart is not a psychological state or a human achievement but a new creation, a higher reality that is a gift, a new being.[10] He uses the patristic distinction between the image and the likeness of God to explain the effects of original sin. Created in the image of God, one has lost the likeness by becoming centered on the self and separated from God as the source of reality. One is still the image of God, but the loss of charity—participation in the life of God—means that one is a caricature of one's true self. To become real is to purify one's heart of illusions which take the shape of fear, anxiety, conflict, ambivalence, self-contradiction, compulsive need, and especially the illusory conviction that one is a god. This conviction has some basis in reality, Merton affirms, since the obscure image of God remains in human freedom as the power of spiritual self-determination. But in its distorted form it appears as a kind of relative omnipotence in which one's own will is supreme.

This "radical psychological claim" is repressed and hidden, even to the conscious self, but becomes apparent in ordinary life, for example, in the tyrannical or martyr parent, the overbearing boss, the clown, the libertine—wherever there is the basic, secret project to elevate oneself and one's freedom over the freedom of other selves. In this spiritual context, the only solution to the dilemma is the purity of heart that is learned from obedience to the "Cross of Truth." One's eyes are opened to reality when perfect love delivers one from selfish projects and illusions to the authentic truth of union with God and with other selves.[11]

This truth, writes Merton, reechoed in the *veritas, verus, vere* of the ancient monastic rules and the writings of the fathers, is not a concept but the existential reality of actual life: "living in the truth." Thus all monastic asceticism is ordered to the recovery of the true self, the liberation of the image of God from encrusted layers of "unlikeness."

> One's true self is the person we are meant to be—the [one] who is free and upright, in the image and likeness of God. The work of recovery of this lost likeness is effected by stripping away all that is alien and foreign to our true selves—shedding the "double garment" of hypocrisy and illusion by which we try to conceal the truth of our misery from ourselves, our brethren and from God.[12]

Thus the monk, in working toward the monastic covenant of charity, works at the truth about the self through humility, or honesty, and self-denial—sweeping out all that is useless and alien. And what is alien? All material, created, temporal things when they are used or sought as ends in themselves. This does not imply a Manichean or gnostic separation, according to Merton, for created things are good. But the monastic fathers envision a true *integration* between matter and spirit that results in freedom from "servility" to things, in freedom from false appearances. It is in this sense that the monastery is the school of liberty.[13]

The Silent Life frames the question of the self in strictly monastic terms, and according to the traditional categories of the monastic fathers. The framework is experiential, as it always is for Merton, as he describes a radical conversion from the fiction, illusion, or untruth of the merely human to the intensity of the life of faith wholly directed to God. But experience here is interpreted almost entirely in traditional terms. The intensity of the monastic life means that in the regular asceticism of humility and obedience the monk becomes really detached from self, anonymous, lost in the God whose transcendent reality finally overcomes the falsity of the old self. The spiritual, and ontological, goal of the monk is a new creation which is the restoration of the full image and likeness to God which is lost in original sin. And the psychological result is liberation. This liberty of the true self is manifested in honesty, self-denial, and especially charity, as well as a maturity which liberates one from servility to things. One moves from the false—mere appearance and illusion—to the truth in which one really lives and so finds the true self, the liberation of the image of God in oneself.

The Silent Life is a powerful apologia for monasticism and its vital meaning and purpose for the interior life of the monk. But the book's power is also such that, for the ordinary Christian, it would seem an impossible, rarified, ancient ideal, far too removed from ordinary experience to have much immediate implication for one living in the world outside the monastery.

Not so "The Inner Experience." This text also deals with the contemplative life, but in a way that is accessible to anyone who has attempted a serious life of prayer, whatever one's official vocation may be. Its language is much more immediate than *The Silent Life,* perhaps because of its many revisions, for the last draft reflects the widened horizons of Merton's later thought. A projected book on the contemplative life, "The Inner Experience" is based on the contrast between the false, illusory self and the contemplative, spiritual, true, or "inner self."

Merton begins by pointing out that most problems of the aspiring contemplative are in fact problems of the illusory, exterior self. Solution of these problems occurs with "the dissolution of this false self." The contemplative, inner self is entirely hidden by the busy activity of the exterior self, which seeks, even in contemplation, its own fulfillment. Paradoxically, genuine contemplation can be found only if the very desire for fulfillment is renounced. This is an enduring problem for Merton: one seeks and must seek, but only by ceasing to seek does one find what one is obscurely looking for. In this text, the spiritual self does not seek fulfillment but only to be and to move, dynamically and spontaneously, in its natural unity in the freedom of God.[14]

Most people are preoccupied with the fictitious character they have given themselves in the world of business, politics, scholarship, religion. Following his theme of the Cartesian ego, Merton

theorizes that one makes objects and even other persons exten-
sions of this self and its projects. Immersed in the world of objects, this self loses its subjectivity even though it may be very
conscious of itself and "aggressively definite in saying 'I.'" It succeeds only in making "contemplative faces at [it]self like a child
in front of a mirror. . . ." One is deluded into believing that "experience of [one]self is an experience of God." In contrast, the
inner self is "like a very shy wild animal" which will appear only
when all is peaceful and untroubled. It responds to no coaxing
or manipulative strategy, to no lure except that of divine freedom. It is not an object or a part of one's being "like a motor
in a car" but one's entire reality, the self that one is "as a living
awareness of itself."

> All that we can do with any spiritual discipline is produce within
> ourselves something of the silence, the humility, the detachment,
> the purity of heart, and the indifference which are required if the
> inner self is to make some shy, unpredictable manifestation of [its]
> presence.[15]

All genuine spiritual experience has within it some element of
the inner self in its depth and incommunicability. But the inner
self is then usually present only in a derivative sense, reminding
one of forgotten depths and of one's own helplessness in exploring them.

Thus, according to Merton, the inner self is beyond the control
of one's conscious striving and will. One cannot confront the inner self directly. Rather, Merton's words suggest the difference
between "active" and "passive" contemplation, or between what
the mystical tradition distinguishes as "active" and "infused"
contemplation, the difference between conscious striving and allowing something to happen to oneself in prayer. The point is
that at this level of prayer, one is counseled only to seek the self-
forgetful virtues and allow the workings of grace to take over, to
let something happen to one in prayer rather than aggressively
trying to *make* something happen. This "letting go" of one's hold

on oneself (a hold previously encouraged by the active pursuit of virtue as an asceticism of "control" of the passions and senses, for example,) is almost a complete reversal of the pattern of the beginning stages of prayer and thus represents a difficult switch of psychological attitude. Merton's image of the inner self as a shy wild animal is very suggestive in this context: one must be very patient and still, melt into the background, so to speak, and simply wait until it appears to the shy "animal" that is the hidden self that *no one is there,* before the inner self will venture briefly into the light and show itself.

The awakening of the inner self, for Merton, is a very subtle yet simple business, similar to the experience described by the Zen masters. Merton was already exploring Zen Buddhism at the time of the later drafts of "The Inner Experience," especially through the writings of D. T. Suzuki, the best-known interpreter of Zen for Western readers. Suzuki had become a friend to Merton through correspondence, and with the permission of his abbot, Merton was allowed to travel to New York to visit him in 1964.

In this passage of "The Inner Experience" one can see one of the special points of Merton's interest in Zen, its interpretation of the Buddhist doctrine of no-self *(anatta).* For Merton inserts an example from Zen as a nearly "clinically perfect" case of what is meant by the awakening of the inner self in the natural order. In his discussion he follows Suzuki in maintaining the purely psychological and even anti-mystical character of Zen, although he comments that the Eastern "mystics," lacking the centuries of theological debate characteristic of the West, may not have reflected analytically on the fine points of their experience but may have indeed experienced the presence of God in what they speak of as knowing the inmost self. Merton acknowledges that Christian theologians generally regard Asian mysticism as natural rather then supernatural, but he observes that the supernatural is possible outside the church.[16] This position is in stark contrast to the first edition of *Seeds of Contemplation,* in which Merton was completely negative about the possibility of authentic mystical experience outside the Catholic Church.

In "The Inner Experience," Merton suggests that the Zen experience, at least, allows observation of the natural operations of the inner self. The example he chooses is an account of *satori,* the moment of highest realization or breakthrough in Zen. He describes *satori* as an inner explosion, a "bursting open of the inner core of the spirit" which "blasts the false self to pieces and leaves nothing" but one's inmost or original self. Zen theory indicates that when one reaches a certain point of inner maturity, the inward pressure is such that any fortuitous word or sound may touch off a revolutionary change in one's whole being. *Satori* is a "sudden, definitive, integral realization of the nothingness of the exterior self and consequently, the liberation of the real self, the inner 'I'." Yet this, Merton cautions, is Western language: the real self, in Zen terms, finally transcends the distinction between self and not-self.[17]

The text Merton chooses is one that Suzuki records, the story of Chao-pien's enlightenment:

Devoid of thought, I sat quietly by the desk in my official room,
With my fountain-mind undisturbed, as serene as water;
A sudden clash of thunder, the mind-doors burst open,
And lo, there sits the old man in all his homeliness.[18]

Merton observes that the state of tranquil reflection is the "natural climate in which the spiritual self may yield up its secret identity." This occurs in a sudden awareness in which the false self is caught in its nakedness and is instantly dispelled as illusion, a pure fiction, a shadow of self-deception. It not only disappears, but is seen never to have been there at all. And the real self becomes transparent in all its reality. The real self is not the ideal, imaginary creature of one's compulsive need for perfection but simply oneself and nothing more, the way one simply is in the eyes of God both in "littleness and ineffable greatness." The phrase, "old man," Merton comments, here means precisely the opposite of the Pauline sense of the term; rather the Zen reference would be analogous to the Pauline "new man."[19]

How does this Zen description relate to Western, Christian tradition? Is Merton suggesting that Zen and Christian experience is really the same thing expressed in different language? Christian mystics also write of the discovery of the inner self, Merton answers, but add an important distinction. While in Zen there is no attempt to go beyond the inner self, in Christianity the inner self is understood as an opening into the awareness of God, as a mirror in which God is seen but which is also revealed to be only the mirror. This metaphorical language, according to Merton, is

> a way of saying that our being somehow communicates directly with the Being of God, Who is "in us." If we enter into ourselves, find our true self, and then pass "beyond" the inner "I," we sail forth into the immense darkness in which we confront the "I AM" of the Almighty.[20]

While the Zen writers are concerned with what is given in experience and might suggest that Christianity simply adds a theological interpretation of the experience, Merton insists on the importance of distinguishing, in agreement with Jewish, Islamic, and Christian traditions, between the being of God and that of the soul. Even though, paradoxically, the inmost self exists in God, "we must know that the mirror is distinct from the image reflected in it. The difference rests on theological faith." Hence, awareness of the inner self can be the consequence of a natural, psychological purification. Awareness of *God* is supernatural participation in and experiential knowledge of the graced light by which God is revealed as present *in* the inner self.[21] Merton insists on a difference between Zen and Christianity that is more than a matter of language.

Yet he cites texts from John Tauler, the fourteenth-century Dominican mystic, and from John of the Cross, his favorite Carmelite mystic and mentor, to demonstrate ways in which Christian contemplatives have described the awakening of the inner self and consequent awareness of God that are similar to Zen accounts. While respecting the important differences of interpretation between Zen and Christianity, Merton's interest is in the *experience* described in the two traditions and he does not so much concern himself with the differences in abstract doctrine or theory. Tauler refers to the inmost "I" as the "ground," the "center," or "apex" of the soul; his imagery of tasting from an "inward fountain" and of a "flash of lightening" are analogous to the poem of Chao-pien. And he maintains the traditional ascetic notions of the purification necessary for the entrance to the inward self: liberation from sense-satisfaction, pleasure-seeking, love of comfort, pride, vanity—even, according to Merton, from "the ordinary flow of conscious and half-conscious sense impressions . . . , the unconscious drives and the clamoring of inordinate passions."[22]

St. John of the Cross describes this liberation of the self in terms of "faith" and the "dark night" of the senses and of the spirit; at the end of the process of ascetic detachment one is released to voyage beyond oneself to God. The final paradox is that God and the soul become as a "single I, . . . as though one person." For Merton, at this point anyone who is fully aware of the depths of one's alienation from the inmost self may find the idea of such union incredible. Yet, he writes, the Christian message, as interpreted by the mystical and spiritual traditions and by the monastic fathers, clearly describes the real possibility of a return from "exile" to "paradise," where one finds one's true self, which is God's presence within.[23]

Merton's use of the theme of exile from paradise is derived from patristic theology—Gregory of Nyssa, for example—and from the desert fathers, who interpreted the sin described in Genesis (2–3) as a fall from contemplative union with God and an exile into multiplicity and exteriority. Thus human beings experience original sin, the loss of the "likeness" to God even as the "image" of God is retained, in the experience of division, alienation, fragmentation, dispersal. The goal of the ascetic life, as the turn to the desert, is the return from exile to the paradise of contemplation in the recovery of a lost identity. Thus Merton writes, in "The Inner Experience," that "our inmost I is the perfect image of God."

> To anyone who has full awareness of our exile from God, our alienation from this inmost self, and our blind wandering in the "regions of unlikeness," this claim can hardly seem believable. Yet it is nothing else but the message of Christ calling us to awake from sleep, to return from exile and find our true selves within ourselves, in that inner sanctuary which is His Temple and His Heaven, and (at the end of the prodigal's homecoming journey) the "Father's House."[24]

In "The Inner Experience," Merton devotes an entire chapter to "Society and the Inner Self," maintaining that the inner self cannot be recovered simply by isolation and introversion or individual self-affirmation in opposition to membership in a group. The inner self is not emptiness or unconsciousness, nor is it what remains when one has turned away completely from exterior reality. It is, rather, related to external things and especially other subjects in an entirely new way, within a deeper, spiritual horizon: things are seen, Zen-like, without affirmation or denial in a kind of concrete intuition that is childlike and simple, an active receptivity and responsiveness. The exterior self looks at everything from an *angle,* a detached or "scientific" attitude which distances one from contact with reality, and is one of the main obstacles to contemplation. (Merton notes that possible exceptions to this are evident in scientists like Einstein and Heisenberg, who possessed a genuine contemplative spirit.)[25]

But in any case, one cannot arrive at inner realization unless one is deeply aware of oneself as related to other persons. The inner self sees the other in an I-Thou relation; and the other is known as a complementary self. One is united with others even in spiritual solitude. For the inner self is inseparable from Christ.

And so the church, the mystical Christ, must be seen as more than a collectivity or a juridical society: the traditional Christian notion of "edification," as the building up of the body of Christ, is the mutual recognition of inner selves. "The awakening of the inner self is purely the work of love and there can be no love where there is not 'another' to love." And this, Merton affirms, is not something pale and without passion but a love in which passion has been purified by selflessness, in which one seeks the good of the other rather than one's own interest or pleasure. While solitude is necessary for freedom, once freedom has been achieved it must be turned to action in "service of a love for which there is no longer subjection or slavery."[26]

Merton develops some of the psychological implications of the false self by speculating that the exterior self is not limited to the conscious level but has its unconscious dimensions as well. There can be a *false* withdrawal to the depths of the exterior self.

> Freud's superego, as an infantile and introjected substitute for conscience fits very well my idea of the exterior and alienated self. It is at once completely exterior and yet at the same time buried in unconsciousness. So too with the Freudian concept of the "id," in so far as it represents an automatic complex of drives toward pleasure or destruction, in response to external stimuli.[27]

In Merton's estimation, Freud's theory helps to explain false mysticism and pseudo-religiosity. Instead of growing into true freedom, one withdraws to the subterranean levels of the exterior self, which are still alienated and subject to external compulsion. In contrast to the freedom and spontaneity of an inner self unpreoccupied with itself, there is a religious fanaticism which is "ponderous" and "obsessive," which lays claim to "magical" insight into others and sees "portentous signs" in external events. Merton describes false religiosity in strong words: it is a "realm of dangerous appetites for command," a "spiritual sensuality"; "dark with obsession," it has "undertones of sex perversion."[28]

The unconscious exterior self has its collective manifestations too. While all religions are meant to guide those who seek the awakening of the inner self, only the highest forms of religious worship succeed in the contemplative awakening of its participants that is real union with God. The lowest form of worship is magical; and in between there are manifold kinds. But most religions only succeed in reaching the collective exterior self. Technological society also has its manifestations of pseudo-spiritual catharsis in its idolatries of state, class, violence. (Today one might add sex to Merton's list of idolatries.) These present a parody of religious mystery in evoking a mere "collective shadow of a 'self.' " Their ersatz interiority is unconscious and results in a "sweet loss of personal responsibility" which can feel like spontaneity. In fact such manifestations are a "pseudo-Christ in which all real selves are lost." Even genuine religion can degenerate, using stimulating agents—drugs, alcohol—to break routine and inhibition. But "the inner self thus released is not necessarily the 'I' but . . . usually the subconscious libido held in check . . . by conscience, habit, . . . fear." The release achieved in this way is material, not spiritual, writes Merton, again using Maritain's language, "an explosion of psychic energy" that may be good or bad according to the circumstances.[29]

In contrast to the false release of these collective manifestations, Merton offers, in "The Inner Experience," authentic alternatives from the religions of the world. The "striving is always the same: the quest for unity, a return to the inmost self united with the Absolute," in which one also seeks the redemption of *all* living beings. The doctrine of detachment and pure love in the *Bhagavad Gita,* for example, like that of the Christian mystics Bernard, Tauler, Fenelon, is one in which the yogi is not an exterior self mirrored in his own ego but rather one who has found his inner self in selfless love. In Christianity, the desert fathers offer the starkest example of the goal of the contemplative quest in their ruthless attempt to dispel any illusions of the false self as they seek "the face of God." But the whole Christian contemplative tradition is one in its search for the quasi-experiential knowledge of God in luminous darkness, the perfection of faith enlightening the inmost self. Such enlightenment is not enjoyment, peace, happiness, nor is it a "sleepy restful embrace of being in a dark, generalized contentment." It is the triumph of divine freedom in the inmost "I," the flash of lightning that is meeting with God.[30]

In "The Inner Experience," Merton lays out the theological foundations for his doctrine of the self. Beginning again with the desert and patristic symbolism of Adam's fall from paradise as a fall from contemplative union with God, he describes the human exile as both from God and from the true self. One no longer recognizes one's inner "face" in the Spirit and in God for this is an identity which is "secret, invisible, incommunicable." Having become dependent on self-observation and self-assertion, one seeks happiness outside oneself. God must die on the cross, leaving the pattern and proof of love in order for humankind to "return to paradise" and recover the self of its true identity. In union and communion with God and with others in the death and resurrection of Christ, the Christian dies a spiritual death in which the inner self rises from death by faith and lives in God. Christianity is thus the rediscovery of paradise, the recovery of the self as another Christ.[31]

Merton bases this theology of the true contemplative self on the ancient christological doctrine of the union of the human and divine natures in the one divine person of Christ. This is the basis for the divinization of the Christian, a favorite theme of the Eastern fathers of the church. Recalling the Greek fathers, Merton describes the Christian as baptized into Christ and as developing the life of divinization through asceticism, charity, and contemplation. He works as well from the New Testament, especially St. Paul, and claims that Pauline thought is pervaded by the idea of contemplation even though the word is never used. For example, Merton interprets passages about "Christ's love which surpasses all understanding" (Eph. 3:19) and "the life of the Spirit in our inmost soul" (I Cor. 2:10–12) as indications of

the hidden presence which awaits one's deliverance from preoccupation with the external, selfish, illusory self. The seeds of this
deliverance are planted in the divided self at baptism but they
will hardly grow unless they are nourished by some form of contemplation in which the reality of baptism is practically and interiorly realized in the self.[32]

Finally, in the last fully developed part of "The Inner Experience," Merton suggests some of the attitudinal consequences of
contemplation and the discovery of the inner self. It is contemplation that engenders in the person a sacred, in contrast to a
secular, attitude. For even religious acts can become secularized
if they are performed in a kind of dependence or servility, for
example, to allay one's anxiety or to obtain social approval. The
sacred attitude is one in which one is not afraid of one's own
inner emptiness.

> There is a subtle but inescapable connection between the "sacred"
> attitude and the acceptance of one's inmost self. The movement of
> recognition which accepts our own obscure and unknown self pro-
> duces the sensation of a "numinous" presence within us. [This is]
> . . . no magic illusion but the real expression of a release of spiritual
> energy, testifying to our own interior reunion and reconciliation
> with that which is deepest in us, and, through the inmost self, with
> the transcendent and invisible power of God. [It] . . . implies hu-
> mility, or full acceptance of all that we have tended to ignore and
> reject in ourselves.[33]

One who develops a sacred attitude overcomes self-hatred and
is able to remain in loneliness, for, paradoxically, loneliness becomes the source of peace and of awareness of the presence of
God. Further, such a person is able to move from inner loneliness
to find God in others; no longer needing to identify other persons
with their sins or judge or condemn them for their actions, one
can help others to put up with themselves, educating them in
confidence by respect until they are brought to the interior quiet
in which they learn to find God in their own poverty. For the

deepest problem in the spiritual life is "acceptance of our hidden and dark self with which we tend to identify all that is evil in us." Merton says that acceptance of this dark self, "respect for the real, in whatever form," is the beginning of awareness of the inmost self. Thus, the ground is prepared so that new life, beyond one's explicit knowledge and conscious control, may begin to grow.[34]

While there is no evidence that Merton was more than casually familiar with the psychological theories of Carl Jung, whose work Merton had read in his student days, his counsel about accepting the "dark self" is similar to Jungian theory about the "shadow" in each personality type and the importance of recognizing in oneself this negative or rejected side of one's personality. Jung holds that if the shadow of the personality is not recognized and accepted, it is never fully developed and becomes the basis for irrational outbursts which one does not understand in oneself, and for the projection of evil or blame or one's own negative qualities onto others.[35]

The unfinished remainder of "The Inner Experience" indicates that Merton intended to deal with some of the standard issues of mystical theology, together with some special contemporary problems, by carrying through the theme of the true and the false selves. Though incomplete, it is a remarkable work in many ways, not least for the light it sheds on the centrality of the "true self" and the meaning of authentic identity in Merton's thought. Not merely a congenial typology, the understanding of the self as the inner or true self is a focal issue around which he sees the whole structure of religious experience and growth toward spiritual maturity.

The Silent Life and "The Inner Experience" reflect a transition in Merton's understanding of the self. *The Silent Life* emphasizes the hidden character of the true self and the positive goal of monastic asceticism—detachment from self-absorption in order that God and the true self may appear in the place empty of self. This is Merton's interpretation of the patristic notion of "purity of heart." And although Merton insists that the patristic doctrine of the image and lost likeness do not refer to psychology but to the ontological level of "new being," he is ineluctably drawn to reflection on the psychological resonances of the doctrine in his emphasis on the *experience* of the contemplative life. Practical realization of the significance of the image which remains even after original sin and the ascetic and contemplative recovery of the lost likeness involves the overcoming of conflict, anxiety, ambivalence, compulsiveness, and the radical, repressed psychological claim that every individual harbors to a kind of omnipotence, a tendency to absolutize oneself. The actualization of the true self through the monastic or contemplative discipline leads to an integration of spiritual aspiration and psychological experience that results in an independence from false appearances, a free dom from servility to things, a new liberty.

In "The Inner Experience," the terms of the discussion are slightly changed from true and false selves to the inner and exterior selves. The hidden, inner self is found only when even the *desire* for spiritual fulfillment can be renounced, a subtle turn which reflects Merton's growing awareness of the radical depths of the false or merely exterior self. For profound self-deception can characterize even those who aspire to religious selflessness: everyone is susceptible to the falsity of "impersonation," imitation of the fictitious character created by the exterior self. Anyone who has had some genuine spiritual experience is aware of this tendency, according to Merton.

In exploring the psychological implications of this depth of falsity, Merton suggests that the exterior self extends to the unconscious level in both individual and collective experience, thus offering an interesting psychological argument for the truth of the inner self as beyond the control of the thinking, willing, superficial self—the ego—and a confirmation of the traditional mystical requirement of passive, in addition to active, purification. This is consonant with his suggestion that it is a new acceptance of the loneliness of one's "dark self" as real and as one's own that is, paradoxically, the beginning of awareness of the inmost self. Merton insists that ascetic purification, like the interior discipline of Zen practice, can only prepare or dispose one to receive, from the outside, as it were, the sudden realization of the inner self, a self that is strangely familiar and ordinary. He is careful to distinguish the natural realization of the inner self in Zen tradition from the supernatural experience of the Christian mystic which goes beyond the inner self to awareness of the presence of God.

Adam's fall and the death and resurrection of Christ provide the theological pattern for the Christian's realization of the restored and new life that is communicated in baptism and experienced in contemplation. The overcoming of the exterior self and discovery of the inner self, and God, entail a union that is so intimate that it is experienced as an *identity* with God. Finally, all of this analysis is given new social emphasis in Merton's affirmation of the essential, though purified relatedness of the inner self to others. Other people are loved in Christ within a new horizon of truth and sympathy that is no longer self-centered or judgmental but which sees in the other a complementary self.

The rather theoretical discussion of *The Silent Life* and even the more experiential "The Inner Experience," based in the ancient Christian theology of the Greek fathers and monastic and mystical traditions, and recovered in their richness in Merton's theology of contemplation, are nevertheless somewhat distant from the experience of ordinary Christians outside the monastery. And they are perhaps rather forbidding in the austerity of the quest they describe. The teachings of these texts can appear to represent a noble but unreachable ideal for the average lay reader, an esoteric experience that is available only within monastery walls. When Merton next takes up the question of the self, it is in the more relaxed, immediate and even casual context of a personal journal. And it is a context that is more familiar to the ordinary Christian because of the immediacy and concreteness of its struggles and concerns.

3

CONJECTURES AT A
TURNING POINT

In *Conjectures of a Guilty Bystander,* published in 1966, there
is evidence of both continuity and change in Merton's thought.
There is continuity in his persistent focus on the question of the
self and radical change because of the wider horizons of thought
and experience that age and extended human contacts brought
to Merton's perceptions of the spiritual and contemplative and
monastic life. Not least important is the presence of a new kind
of doubt and struggle in Merton's personal life. And the era of
the Second Vatican Council brought innumerable questions
about renewal, *aggiornamento,* the need for updating the old
forms and structures of Catholic Christian life, including the
forms of monastic life.

Chief among the questions for Merton was that which is symbolized in *The Constitution on the Church in the Modern World
(Gaudium et Spes)* of Vatican II, the question of the Christian's
embodiment and expression of a more positive relation to the
world of which the church and the monastery are an integral
part. The traditions of monasticism and contemplation as explicit structures of withdrawal from the world and from the patterns of ordinary life, as from either a positively evil environment
or at least from a context which distracts the Christian from the
single-minded life of prayer, were the subject of both external
and internal criticism and change in the monasticism of the

1960s. And while some of the changes were reasonable accommodations to the changed context of culture and society—for example, the simplification of monastic habits from the complicated medieval clothes of a past era—some of the changes or proposed changes seemed to Merton to question more deeply the essential meaning of a dedicated or solitary life of prayer. Merton's personal life also went through a serious upheaval toward the end of this period. In 1966, he fell in love with a nurse he met during a hospital stay. The story is sensitively handled in the Mott biography. Mott concludes that the experience, while a painful one for Merton and full of foolish indiscretions and impositions on his friends, was an important and transforming experience for him, even an experience of grace. For it was demonstrable proof to Merton that he could really love and be loved.[1]

Merton's reflections on the theme of the true self in *Conjectures of a Guilty Bystander* reflect this period of confusion and ambivalence as well as its heady euphoria. The book itself derives from notebooks Merton began to keep in 1956. A collection of reflections, sketches, metaphors, comments on reading and events, it presents a radically new tone in contrast to the writings of Merton's earlier periods. While most of his published writing of the time (1956–66) is, as Rice says, "entirely 'Christian,' in fact Catholic in the specific sense," this journal demonstrates the expanding horizons of Merton's reading and thinking: Protestant theology, existential philosophy and psychology, new Christian and literary perspectives. Barth, Bonhoeffer, Teilhard de Chardin, Gandhi, J. A. T. Robinson, Heidegger, Sartre, and the new Latin American poets are among the subjects of his commentary. And his concerns are clearly with the world outside the monastery: the possibility of war, racial conflict and violence in the United States, reports of the Holocaust, Marxism and the questions it raises about traditional religion, nuclear tests, and expanding technology. And the intensification of Merton's enduring interest in the spiritual traditions of the East and Islamic mysticism (Sufism) signify a new breadth and openness in his vision of the contemplative life.[2]

Conjectures of a Guilty Bystander, taken from notebooks begun in 1956 but completed only in 1965, belongs to what Merton calls the fourth stage in his writing and his life at Gethsemani. In 1955, he was named Master of the Choir Novices, a position of great responsibility in the monastery. In this work, as he dealt with the sometimes troubled young men who came to enter the Cistercian Order, he saw the need for someone trained in pastoral psychology in the monastery to screen applicants and to offer psychological counsel to the monks. He himself dabbled a bit in psychology and psychoanalysis, and he learned to give the Rorschach test. He read Karen Horney, agreed with her criticism of Freud, and apparently attempted a self-analysis in the context of his own "instability crisis," that is, his attraction to other religious orders which would allow him more solitude. Merton had a difficult and humiliating public encounter with a celebrated psychoanalyst at a meeting in 1956 at Collegeville, Minnesota, which suggested to him that he was himself "in bad shape," "neurotic," and that his interest in becoming a hermit might be "pathological."[3] It was a turbulent period, yet one which Merton struggled through and emerged from in apparent mental and spiritual health, as the finished text of *Conjectures,* one of his most powerful books, testifies.

The title of the journal recalls an essay, "Letter to an Innocent Bystander," in Merton's 1961 *Behavior of Titans,* just as the contents of *Conjectures* recall its themes.[4] The "bystander" refers to those who, like Merton himself, are intellectuals and believe that their innocence in the face of world crisis is preserved by their position as detached observers, on a plane above politics. In the essay he argues sharply against any such rejection of responsibility through nonparticipation or mere intellectual resistance. For the bystander is not innocent. In *Conjectures* Merton further focuses the idea on himself: a monk is one whose situation "inevitably makes one something of a bystander." But the tone of this book is less acerbic than the earlier essay. For Merton believes that the solitary indeed may have some important wisdom that the world needs.

> To be a solitary but not an individualist: concerned not with merely perfecting one's own life (this, as Marx saw it, is an indecent luxury and full of illusion.) One's solitude belongs to the world and to God. Are these just words?

> Solitude has its own special work: a deepening of awareness that the world needs. A struggle against alienation. True solitude is deeply aware of the world's needs. It does not hold the world at arm's length.[5]

The guilty bystander may have something of the "night spirit" and the "dawn breath"—the silence, the receptivity, the rest—that human nature requires to be itself and regenerate its life.[6]

There is a new sympathy for those outside the monastery in *Conjectures of a Guilty Bystander.* The pious hostility and suspicion of the world, characteristic of the early Merton, have disappeared.

> In Louisville, at the corner of Fourth and Walnut, in the center of the shopping district, I was suddenly overwhelmed with the realization that I loved all those people, that they were mine and I theirs, that we could not be alien to one another even though we were total strangers. It was like waking from a dream of separateness, of spurious self-isolation in a special world, the world of renunciation and supposed holiness. . . . This sense of liberation from an illusory difference was such a relief and such a joy to me that I almost laughed out loud. . . . I have the immense joy of being . . . a member of a race in which God Himself became incarnate. . . . There is no way of telling people that they are all walking around shining like the sun.[7]

This surely is one of the most often remarked passages in the writing of Thomas Merton. And it has surely appeared to many interpreters as the explicit turning point in Merton's religious experience. But as Michael Mott points out, Merton's inclusion of this 1958 passage in *Conjectures* is closely related in time to his writing of the prose-poem *Hagia Sophia,* to his interest in the Bible's Book of Proverbs with its feminine figure of Wisdom, and to a dream that Merton had recently had and which he recorded in his private journal about a young Jewish girl whose name was "Proverb." Mott relates all of this to another passage in Merton's private journal from the exact time that deals specifically with his relationship to *women* and his reflection that while none of the *women* he saw in the street that day in Louisville was particularly beautiful, each had, nevertheless, a secret beauty. By his vow of chastity, Merton notes, he was married to what is most true in all the women of the world.[8]

The biographer comments on his own careful research into the exact context of the famous passage in *Conjectures:*

> For me, it was not any moment of vision in the streets of Louisville that changed Merton's orientation entirely, but the gradual working out of the deep and disturbing themes in *Hagia Sophia.* . . . It is perhaps the most revealing single piece of writing Merton did—revealing, yet hidden.[9]

The deep and disturbing themes in *Hagia Sophia* deal with the feminine, the figure of Holy Wisdom, "my sister," and with the Blessed Virgin Mary. These figures are all related to the themes of God the Creator as mother and the image of Jesus as mother, both interpreted as an invisible fecundity. In a startling and almost prescient figure, given Merton's later tumultuous love affair with a nurse he met while recovering from surgery in a hospital, in *Hagia Sophia,* Merton describes being awakened "out of languor and darkness, out of helplessness" by a nurse in a hospital. It was the morning of July 2, the feast of the Visitation of Mary, the mother of Jesus, to Elizabeth, the mother of John the Baptist:

> It is like being awakened by Eve. It is like being awakened by the

Blessed Virgin. It is like coming forth from primordial nothingness and standing in clarity, in Paradise.

In the cool hand of the nurse there is the touch of all life, the touch of Spirit.

Thus Wisdom cries out to all who will hear . . . and she cries out particularly to the little, to the ignorant and the helpless.

Who is more little, who is more poor than the helpless man who lies asleep in his bed without awareness and without defense?[10]

In the poem, God enters creation as Sophia, as "tenderness, mercy, virginity, the Light, the Life considered as passive, as received, as given," as Gift and Spirit. In Mott's contextual interpretation of the celebrated "Louisville vision" passage in *Conjectures of a Guilty Bystander,* Merton's new perception of love for other people, even ordinary people in the world of busy shoppers, even women (an early symbol of Merton's general distrust of the world and a specific symbol of temptation and distraction from God) is particularized with dramatic intensity in the feminine, the woman, as someone he could love.

However, this new realization ultimately does not change the value of solitude for Merton but intensifies it. Although it brings a new kind of struggle into his life, it eventually deepens his sense that his own solitude belongs to others, especially through his writing. "It is because I am one with them that I owe it to them to be alone, and when I am alone they are not 'they' but my own self."[11]

The earlier sharp distinctions which Merton had drawn between the natural and the supernatural are dramatically changed. Where once he had seen the monastic life as a haven of supernatural purity in contrast to the corruption of the world, he now writes with awareness of the "ghetto" possibilities of the monastery—"when it turns in on itself, interpreting interpretations of interpretations." He writes that there is no ghetto spirit in St. Benedict, whose vision was broad and open. The spirit and letter

of his Rule do not counsel "locking doors and windows" against
the world but rather point to the importance of discernment between the useful and the useless in order to glorify God in all
things. "The monk must *see Christ* in the pilgrim and stranger
who come from the world. . . . "[12]

Further, Merton states as a principle the idea that *some* natural
appetites are God's will: "we cannot live in the truth if we automatically suspect all desires and pleasures. It is humility to accept our humanity. . . . " It is usually better, he says, to do the
simply human and ordinary thing than to attempt to perform
like an angel; there is no need to reject everything that is not
overtly pious.

> For others who are human enough to be ascetics without losing any
> of their humanity, it is all right to risk things that seem inhuman.
> For one as deficient and self-conscious as I am, the ordinary ways
> are safer. They are not just an evasion to be tolerated; they are a
> more perfect way.[13]

Merton cites Ananda Coomaraswamy, a Hindu philosopher
whose work he had used extensively in his Columbia thesis, to
the effect that actions performed naturally are sacred or profane
according to one's level of awareness, but that anything "done
unnaturally is essentially and irrevocably profane." Thus, as Merton notes the increasing use of heavy machinery on the monastery
farms, he points out that while technology is not evil in itself, it
can be a serious problem if it destroys the natural and deadens
the human spirit which grace is meant to transform. No mere
"supernatural intention" can sanctify a frustrated spirit. Merton's
enduring love for nature, especially the countryside around the
monastery, as a created and sacramental goodness is expanded
in a new way to include *human* nature as well.[14]

A final dimension of Merton's more nuanced understanding
of the nature/supernature distinction touches on work and politics. He writes that too simplistic an interpretation of the nature/
grace distinction can lead one to think that only religious or pious
acts are supernatural and that these represent only momentary

rescues from the profane routine of ordinary life, that Christian social action is a kind of "escalator" to unworldliness. But this, he says, is to ignore the inherent spiritual capacity of material things. Christian social action rather envisions ordinary human work as spiritual, or searches for those conditions under which work can recover the holy quality which makes it a source of spiritual as well as material well-being. The doctrine of the Incarnation, Merton urges, implies the obligation to bring all persons to a level appropriate to their dignity in Christ; it means that Christian political action can be "an expression of spiritual responsibility." It would then include distinctive emphases on the *human* (over collective and productive concerns), the *personal* (the realm of freedom, friendship, creativity, spirit), and *wisdom* (a contemplative or sapiential view in which life is seen in its wholeness, the ancient view in which traditional cultures were rooted in the patterns of nature and the cosmos, a wisdom immanent in world and society).[15]

This understanding of the authentic nature of politics, as entailing the human, the personal, and wisdom is striking in the political context of the cold war of the late 1950s. Among Merton's widening circle of correspondents at this time was Boris Pasternak, whose novel *Dr. Zhivago* Merton had read and deeply appreciated as a triumph of the human spirit, in its natural and Christian intuition of wisdom. When Pasternak was named as the winner of the Nobel Prize for Literature in 1958, Merton was a perceptive analyst of the storm of political controversy that arose, as many Russian critics denounced Pasternak as disloyal to Russia and many Western critics seized the opportunity to read Pasternak's work as a simple criticism of communism, especially of the purges and the other horrors of the Stalin regime. Merton interpreted the novel as a challenge both to the totalitarian collectivism of Russia and to the materialist collectivism of the West. *Dr. Zhivago* was, for him, deeply Christian, sacramental, and even liturgical, but not in any formal, hieratic, ritualistic sense.[16]

Pasternak's work "reveals the cosmic liturgy of Genesis," Merton writes. In the novel, Pasternak challenges communism with "life itself," in a natural and almost primitive way. He is "a prophet of the original, cosmic revelation."

> It is as artist, symbolist and prophet that *Zhivago* stands most radically in opposition to Soviet society. He himself is a man of Eden, of Paradise. He is Adam, and therefore also, in some sense, Christ. Lara is Eve, and Sophia (the cosmic Bride of God) and Russia.[17]

Merton continues to extend Maritain's personalism and metaphysics of spirit—a central part of his early equipment as a literary critic—in new ways as he explores the feminine figure of Wisdom, present at the creation. To Merton, Lara in *Zhivago* was like "sister life," "sophianic." Wisdom and the purity of creation, the natural as opposed to the artificial, are related to the theme of the true self in Merton's work at this period.

This changed context of theological understanding is obviously tied to important changes in Merton's own experience. While *Conjectures* is not as personal a statement as his earlier monastic journal, *The Sign of Jonas,* it does provide indications of new directions in Merton's life. The long struggle with his identity as a monk and as a writer has almost disappeared and a new and creative strength emerges. The sly suggestions of his "shadow" that he compose a series of sentences beginning, "You think you are a monk, but . . . " is followed by a comment that echoes some of the themes of Bonhoeffer's *Letters and Papers from Prison:*

> Perhaps I am stronger than I think. Perhaps I am even afraid of my strength, and turn it against myself, thus making myself weak, . . . secure, . . . guilty. Perhaps I am most afraid of the strength of God in me. . . . [18]

Merton writes that he thinks he may die soon, and that the habitual awareness of death makes him realize the futility of his cares, the chief of which is concern over his work as a writer. But he no longer feels very guilty about his writing, even though it is a concern which keeps his "self" in view and hampers his freedom. For, he says, "I know by experience that without this care and salutary work I would be much more in my own way." And he points to a particular change in his "own inner climate: the coming of autumn," a change that works itself out in "deep unheavals of impatience, resentment, disgust," despite his natural joy and love of life. And it is not death or just the body that is speaking in this new mood but an unfulfilled possibility that is frightening because it contains the question, "Who are you when you do not exist?"[19] The search for a kind of non-identity continues, but is accompanied by a forbidding fear. Perhaps the answer to the question of the self was drawing nearer.

The changed horizons of Merton's thought and experience are similarly reflected in his discussions of the self. The tone of the existentialist philosophers he has been reading is more pervasive, and his analyses take a more definite psychological turn. He comments that at one time religious people opposed psychoanalysis because it undermined "a complacent and evasive ethic of good intentions" by unmasking the brutal, selfish, and greedy unconscious. In fact, Merton suggests, psychoanalysis could be of service to Christianity not only through its help in individual reintegration but also by casting its critical light on the sort of "kind" and "loving" action that results in real inhumanity.

In Barthian terms, Merton describes the religion of those whose attempts to become holy easily terminate in the self and not in God. The wish for approval, for certitude, and mere peace with oneself and God, is "anathema to true Christianity" and is the meaning of St. Paul's anger with "the Law." "Such religion," he writes, "is not saved by good intentions." Genuine religion (if it even can be called "religion") is born from God and "from the devastation of our 'trivial' self and all our plans for our self, even though they be plans for a holy self, a pure self, a loving, sacrificing self." [20]

Merton relates to the problem of the self Gabriel Marcel's observation about the infidelity of the artist who works to achieve effects for which he or she is already well known:

We are all too ready to believe that the self that we have created out of our more or less inauthentic efforts to be real in the eyes of others is a 'real self.' We even take it for our identity. Fidelity to such a non-identity is of course infidelity to our real person, which is hidden in mystery.[21]

Merton has become as astute analyst of religious psychology in the course of his own personal struggles with his monastic superiors and with himself. Life, he writes, is a struggle for the truth, a truth that is already possessed in the life that is given at creation but which, paradoxically, is won only through struggle. The monk's particular temptation is to abdicate the struggle in a passive sort of obedience which is nothing less than a refusal to live. While evil and falsity are inevitable in every life, one cannot simply resign oneself to them. "God demands of us a creative consent, in our deepest and most hidden self, the self we do not experience everyday, and perhaps never experience, though it is always there."[22]

What this creative consent might be is indicated in two extended discussions of the real and illusory selves in *Conjectures*. The first is a set of reflections on suicide and why the present time is a suicidal age. Merton writes that the tendency toward suicide is most prevalent among the affluent precisely because the affluent can have almost everything they want. Yet self-respect, love, faith, and peace cannot be had on demand. And this is the problem: American culture teaches people that they can have whatever they really want. So persons are trained to think of themselves as completely autonomous selves, as really having unlimited possibilities. One is "as a god"—and anything is within reach. But the things that can be had easily are not satisfying. And in fact the things one really needs—meaning, authenticity, love—cannot be had through one's own volition, one's desire to grasp them. No ingenuity can "buy" them, not even asceticism, self-help, or religious techniques. The things we really need only come as gifts, and openness is the condition for receiving these gifts. And openness, Merton holds, requires a willingness to give up one's self-image.

In order to be open we have to renounce ourselves, in a sense we have to *die* to our image of ourselves, our autonomy, our fixation on our self-willed identity. We have to be able to relax the psychic and spiritual cramp which knots us in the painful, vulnerable, helpless "I" that is all we know as ourselves.[23]

Merton writes that despair is caused by the paralyzing incapacity to undo the knot, for as the realization dawns that one is "knotted up on *nothing*" and yet one continues to affirm this "nonentity" over against all else, "frustration becomes absolute." One exists only as a denial in a pitiful, makeshift identity. While in some obscure way the despairing individual may intend a kind of noble protest against a destructive situation, one can also justify or rationalize to oneself a total interior refusal. Then one builds a "final identity out of cramp, resentment, and negation." For "the chronic inability to relax this cramp begets despair." In order to destroy the knot, one destroys oneself. Thus it is imperative to "learn to say 'no' to the cramp, and 'yes' to everything else" before it is too late.[24] How does one do this?

Merton's interpretation of illusory autonomy in this context is that it is essentially a refusal of faith. While such faith is not necessarily a theological or specifically Christian faith, neither is it mere "faith in life." It is rather "the natural readiness, the openness, the humility, the self-forgetfulness" which enables one to *"renounce absolute demands,* give up the intransigent claim to perfect autonomy, and *believe in life."* This attitude of faith would include the ability to take risks, to venture into the unknown, and to trust that life will provide for one. In a society, however, where the mass media and politics are so focused on crisis and violence that everyone is defensive and suspicious, the only explicit remedy is to search for faith in God as a gift and be willing to suffer and wait to receive. Such waiting "in great indigence and peril" implies the recognition that one is not alone, that one's life and death are not just one's "own business."[25]

Finally, Merton understands the temptation to despair as entailing its own possibilities for hope and reversal because it forces one to a choice. Persons *"always* have the strength to choose life," he writes, unless they are so destroyed as to no longer be their real selves at all. The only tragedy is the *"needless* and arbitrary" refusal of hope because it comes from a source other than the self. One on the brink of suicide may be on the brink of a miracle. And if one who is so rescued understands the situation, one's ideas of defeat and fulfillment would be totally revised; one would begin to live as a different self, having the humility to receive from an unknown source. This different self is in "no strange supernatural state" but merely "in the ordinary way of human existence." The present age is suicidal precisely because, in believing the image of society created by the mass media, it has forgotten "the ordinary human mode of life." And Merton adds that those who embrace a creative social dissent from this artificial image created by society have an intuitive sense of openness to these ordinary, providential gifts.[26]

Merton no longer thinks in the natural/supernatural terms of his earlier writing. He seems to be searching for a category that points to the depth of the natural or the ordinary, the order of creation, a category that would be less extrinsic and artificial than the "supernatural" but not merely the common or banal. The appropriate theological notion seems to be a form of providence or the grace of creation itself. Merton's criticism of "the world" is no less sharp than before, as in his insightful commentaries on the mass media and the "American myth" of a people who refuse to recognize their own, sometimes ugly, history. But now his criticism is focused on the world as a set of artificial constructions that mask and destroy intrinsic and natural human resources. It is a world that does not so much call for a redeeming religious superstructure as one that needs to be rescued from layers of distorting encrustation and recovered in its pristine, natural character, its goodness.[27]

Merton's second discussion of the self in *Conjectures* follows on an autobiographical comment about his own writing career, which he describes as a "stupid fiction." He reports that he does not wonder if his writing days are over; he simply does not care where they are. He tells himself that the point is to stop trying to adjust to the fact that "night will come and the work will end," and to simply give what he has without reflecting on it. For "adjusting" is an illusion; one takes oneself too seriously as an isolated, autonomous self, like Descartes's thinking subject which is real because it is proved through its own clear ideas. It is irresponsible to start

> with one's ego-identity and to try to bring that identity to terms with external reality by thinking, and then, having worked out practical principles, to act on reality from one privileged autonomous position—in order to bring it into line with an absolute good we have arrived at by thought.[28]

This attempt at perfect control manifests the false or aggressive autonomy by which one mistakes one's interpretation of the real for reality and so "responds" to nothing. One either chooses a servile submission to facts or a rebellion which simply denies the facts in defending the ego. Such adjustment is a futile "system of ambivalences" around a contingent ego trying to make itself absolute.

In these passages of *Conjectures of a Guilty Bystander,* Merton is clearly concerned, as always, about his own work, his writing. He usually had several different writing projects going at once and his own identity was closely tied to his work as a writer, even as he struggled to see his own identity as more deeply tied to the work of being a monk. He is critical of any psychological theory that would counsel mere "adjustment" to reality and is searching for a way to let go or get free of the planning, projecting, imperious ego. The answer, he suggests, is to simply give what one has in one's work without too much reflection. In the thought patterns of his earlier master's thesis, it is the inherent virtue in the artist which emerges in the work. An attempt to control or manipulate one's work results in an artificiality such that the work fails in the end. The work itself has no integrity and the person of the artist is corrupted in the attempt at rigid control.

Thus he reflects that respect for other persons and their needs, and for oneself, means turning to the "deep mystery of our own identity," beyond the "superficial ego—this cramp of the imagination." This respect means going back to the beginning and recognizing in oneself a simple affirmation, a "primordial yes" which is not at one's disposal or open to inspection and is rarely even experienced as real. It is the recognition that one's own being is not an affirmation of the "limited self, but the 'yes' of Being itself."

> Where do "I" come in? Simply in uniting the "yes" of my own freedom with the "yes" of Being that already *is* before I have a chance to choose. . . . There is nothing to adjust. There is reality, and there is free consent. There is the actuality of one "yes." In this actuality no question of "adjustment" remains and the ego vanishes.[29]

To ignore this primordial reality is to live in a constant series of adjustments; it is to walk a tightrope over an "abyss of nothingness." And both the adjustment and the tightrope are fictions. "The abyss of nothingness is, in fact, the abyss of Being." In Christian terms, Merton says, the gift of such pure affirmation can only be arrived at "in Christ," in an abandoned and trusting consent to the "yes" of Christ to the Father's will.

Interestingly, Merton closes his discussion of this primordial affirmation as Christian with a self-critical, apologetic comment that the great flaw in his own life and writing is that he is so seldom conscious of the meaning of his own Christianity. "But, on the other hand," he writes:

> my fidelity to Christ demands that I avoid too facile a recourse to Christian unction and pious phrases. I will continue to do what I can with the little faith I have, because to pretend I had more would do no honor to the truth. It would, in fact, be only a fraudulent "adjustment."[30]

One might conjecture that the guilty bystander's theological vision of the true and illusory selves is changing radically. The familiar Christian phrases rest a bit uneasily on the more existentialist and psychological insights Merton is exploring. And his own experience is leading him to a different sort of Christian understanding. Merton's long-held conviction that some form of contemplation means access to the experienced realization of redemptive union with God and to the identity of the real self is suggested in new terms in *Conjectures of a Guilty Bystander*.

In some of the most original and engaging passages of this book there is the recurrent theme of the hidden wisdom of the *point vierge,* the "blind sweet point" where "all wisdom seeks to collect and manifest itself." This point is marked by the first sounds of the birds at dawn "when the Father in perfect silence opens their eyes." Wisdom is an ineffable innocence, knowledge of the secret that paradise is everywhere. The apex of the spirit is "the center of our nothingness where, in apparent despair, one meets God—and is found completely" in God's mercy, a point of emptiness that is free from sin, illusion, the fantasies and brutalities of the false self. It is God's name written in one's poverty.[31]

> It is like a pure diamond, blazing with the invisible light of heaven. It is in everybody, and if we could see it we would see these billions of points of light coming together in the face and blaze of a sun that would make all the darkness and cruelty of life vanish completely. . . . I have no program for this seeing. It is only given. But the gate of heaven is everywhere.[32]

This cosmic, natural wisdom is related to Merton's opening reflection in *Conjectures of a Guilty Bystander* on Karl Barth's report of his dream about examining Mozart in theology. Mozart, Merton comments, had rejected Protestantism as being "all in the head," as not knowing the meaning of the *agnus dei qui tollis peccata mundi* (the "lamb of God who takes away the sins of the world.") Barth says that in his dream he attempted to make the examination a favorable one by alluding to Mozart's masses. "But," Barth reports, "Mozart did not answer a word." Merton was moved by the report of the dream, had wanted to write to Barth about it, and suggests that Barth's playing of Mozart each day before working on his theology was an attempt to

awaken "the hidden sophianic Mozart in himself," the essential
wisdom that harmonizes with "the divine and cosmic music and
is saved by love, yes, even by eros," by a child, the lamb of God.[33]

Wisdom, Merton says, is also the work of the monk, who is
the "true philosopher:" the highest wisdom, beyond reasoning
and clear understanding, is grasped by the monk as a totality.
Or better, one who is truly wise is seized by wisdom itself. One
who is wise abandons all effort to seize wisdom and enters into
a new dimension of existence in which all divisions—subject and
object, ends and means—are entirely different, or disappear entirely. Thus the monk, and any serious Christian, is committed
to a goal that cannot be achieved and realizes finally that even
fidelity to a religious ideal does not meet the inscrutable call of
God's love. Ideology, Merton, comments, may be necessary for
beginners, but maturity entails its renunciation in a form of life
in which the separate realities of, for example, poetry and philosophy disappear into the "ordinary acts of life." Ordinary activities, "eating, sleeping, walking . . . become philosophical acts
which grasp the ultimate principles of life in life itself and not
in abstraction." Merton believes that it is from this experience
of the unified life that the enigmatic aphorisms of the Asian contemplatives and the Christian saints come, as does the poetry of
the Zen masters. And he adds that sometimes this unification
of life and worship appears to lack any explicit religious quality.
It is the natural, but newly recovered, wisdom of creation.[34]

What is this supremely ordinary quality that Merton sought
to express? "In a Zen koan," he writes, "someone says that an
enlightened man is not one who seeks Buddha or finds Buddha,
but simply an ordinary man *who has nothing left to do.*" And yet
the issue is not one of merely stopping or doing nothing. The
issue is one of maturity: the person "who is ripe discovers that
there was never anything to be done from the very beginning."
This quality is expressed, for Merton, in his interpretation, following Maritain, of Aquinas' doctrine of creation. This teaching,
Merton says, begins from a direct intuition into the act of being

as "an act of contemplation and philosophical wisdom," not as the result of rational analysis. It is a gift given to children and to simple people of the experience of God's presence within one's own act of being. And the gift involves the challenge of "increasing the intensity and the quality of my act of existence by the free response I make to life." The changed Merton adds that personal being is given not as a source of affliction, but as an access to "joy, growth, creativity and fulfillment."[35]

It is this theology of wisdom and spirit that Merton seeks to articulate around the notion of the true and illusory selves in *Conjectures of a Guilty Bystander*. He is attempting to retrieve, in his life and writing, and in a new historical and cultural setting, the essential and common vision of the monastic and contemplative traditions of the West and of the East as well. This retrieval includes a new and generous sense of openness to and compassion for the world, for all its peoples, and for all its spiritual traditions. He searches for the experience, before and beyond abstraction and technique, of union with God and with others that is born of solitude. Such an experience involves the active casting off of the constant illusions of the false self as one moves into the more receptive, passive, and purifying truth of contemplation. The true self emerges as a kind of unselfconscious non-identity that is nevertheless completely natural, ordinary, personal.

Merton's implicit criticism in *Conjectures* of his own earlier interpretation of the nature/supernature distinction entails a new recognition on his part of the inherent, natural, cosmic wisdom in creation itself. His psychological critique of the religion of the mere "good intention" or "supernatural intention" involves an insight into the false sense of autonomy that it encourages; one is led to imagine that one's religious life is in the control of the thinking, willing self. But the ancient contemplative traditions, like modern psychology, and contemporary existentialism all witness to the falsity of such autonomous control in relation both to the experience of God and to the knowledge of the self.

In religious terms, Merton points out that one cannot come to God through the sheer force of discipline and willing, but only in letting oneself be found by God; this is the traditional notion of passive purification and infused contemplation. In psychological terms, it is only as one releases oneself, usually with the aid of an experienced guide or director, into awareness of the unknown depths of the self that one comes to self-knowledge. In a Jungian framework, this involves knowledge and acceptance of the dark or shadow side of the self, the self which one's conscious ego rejects. Both the religious and psychological perspectives entail acknowledgment of one's essential relatedness and need to receive from sources outside the self, over against the imagined autonomy and rational control of the empirical self.

This essential receptivity is a kind of faith in which one discovers that life itself contains the resources of integrity and maturity and strength. In letting go one's fixed notions, even of religious ideals, one comes to a childlike wisdom that penetrates to the cosmic heart of things in a simplicity and liberty achieved or, rather, given as the goal of the contemplative search. Merton seeks to express this wisdom, a kind of seeing of all things in God and in Christ, in a new language, an ordinary, nontechnical, symbolic language suited to his own experience and to that of the ordinary Christians for whom he writes.

> It is slowly . . . that I work my life into another dimension . . . and there is a growing liberty from the succession of events and experiences. It seems to me that they become less and less *my* experiences. They are more and more woven into the great pattern of the whole experience of [humankind] and even something quite beyond all experience. I am less aware of myself simply as this individual who is a monk and writer, and who, as monk and writer, does this, or writes that. It is my task to see and speak for many, even when I seem to be speaking only for myself.[36]

An intensely personal and compelling theological vision emerges from Merton's apparently casual, but in fact carefully crafted aphoristic reflections in *Conjectures of a Guilty Bystander*.

They are reflections collected in the turbulent years of the racial crisis in the United States, the heightening nuclear crisis and Merton's own impassioned writing on these issues. His involvement in the peace movement at this time brought him into sharp conflict with his superiors and with members of the Roman Catholic hierarchy and for a time he was forbidden to write on the subject of peace. In the midst of these intensely involving activities, in his most "activist" period, the haunting question of the self found a new answer in the vision and the experience of wisdom.

Merton's personal search for wisdom also finds a new wholeness and universality in the context of the openness to the world initiated in the Catholic Church by the Second Vatican Council. The world is no longer seen as evil or as a distraction from the single-minded search for God in prayer, but rather as the environment created by God for human beings that contains its own wisdom, its own joy. This wisdom of creation has been covered over, hidden, distorted by the artificial structures and systems of church and society in a way that parallels the concealed unity of the true or inner self. This is the true self that is hidden beneath the falsity and illusions of the empirical or exterior ego, the false self that one creates for oneself in the social roles that entail continual projection of artificiality, aggression, and competition.

In a new way Merton suggests, in *Conjectures of a Guilty Bystander,* the close connection between the self and society, the social framework of both the development of the false self and of the recovery or discovery of the true, inner self. The false self is an artificial construction that is derived in the context of the various social myths propagated by the mass media and the culture it creates of crisis, fear, consumption, and competition. The discovery of the true, inner self takes place, as Merton has consistently held, through the contemplation taught by the "traditions of wisdom" of the religions of the world. But it is a contemplation that is no longer seen strictly in terms of withdrawal from the world. It is, rather, a contemplation that is in the world as the self's natural environment and home. It is a contemplation that seeks the wisdom of creation itself. It is a contemplation that requires, nevertheless, discernment, criticism, and often a creative dissent on the part of those who are called to search for the presence of God in prayer. Such persons will then be able to give the fruits of their contemplation to the world in love. For the world needs something of the "night air" and "dawn breath" that those who are in touch with traditions of wisdom and spirit can offer.

Merton's new universality, born of his own involvement in the social issues of the 1960s in the United States, his wide-ranging correspondence with other thinkers, writers, and ordinary Christians, and his voracious reading, is leading him to a new breadth and universality in his understanding of the religious quest. And in the context of this new openness, his distinctive theological vision of the self is to find new and further inspiration from his intensified study of the religious traditions of Asia.

4

THE WISDOM OF THE SELF: LEARNING FROM THE EAST

The last section of *Conjectures of a Guilty Bystander* is entitled, in a phrase from a Zen koan, "The Madman Runs to the East." And indeed the last years of Merton's life involve an Asian pilgrimage, first in study and then in actual travel. In 1965, Merton began to live almost entirely as a hermit in a wooded area about a mile from the main buildings of the monastery at Gethsemani. It was there that he spent most of the three remaining years of his life until he left for Asia in the fall of 1968. The last years were not simply quiet, however.

The topics of war and peace, violence and nonviolence, already apparent in *Conjectures of a Guilty Bystander,* become more central as the focus of Merton's thinking and writing. Just as he had been a conscientious objector in World War II, in these last years he protested the war in Viet Nam. In 1965 he addressed an open letter on peace and war to the American Catholic hierarchy and, in Rice's phrase, entered into a kind of guerilla warfare for peace. With his friends and correspondents, Dorothy Day and Daniel Berrigan, he was among the few well-known American Catholics to take an early and open stand against the war, a subject on which his sharpest polemical skills were employed in a steady campaign.

But if the violence of humankind was one deep concern, it was matched by his continued concern for the interior peace of human beings. Through his study of Eastern and Islamic religious traditions, Merton found new insight into this enduring concern, as the problem of the self. Merton's fascination with Eastern religions dates from his early student days at Columbia, when an Indian classmate and friend not only introduced him to some of the Hindu traditions but also encouraged him to read, for the first time, some of the Christian mystics—St. Augustine, for example. Merton's last years were marked by an intensified study of Asian religions that went beyond popular Western curiosity. While his studies represented serious scholarship under the advice of several recognized experts with whom he corresponded, his work also went beyond scholarship in his own personal and practical engagement.[1]

No brief essay better unites the dominating themes of Merton's last years than the touching and enigmatic "Day of a Stranger." From his hermitage in the woods, he is conscious of the passage overhead of the daily jet from Florida to Chicago, its passengers suspended for a time with cocktails in a "contemplation that *gets you somewhere!*" He is aware as well of another plane, an SAC bomber that passes over each day, a "metal bird with a scientific egg in its breast." Both planes and the worlds they represent remind him that he lives in the woods because he is "free not to be a number," that "there is, in fact, a choice."

> In an age when there is much talk about "being yourself," I reserve to myself the right to forget about being myself, since in any case there is very little chance of my being anybody else. Rather it seems to me that when one is too intent on "being himself" he runs the risk of impersonating a shadow.[2]

In the same ironic tone of much of his later poetry, Merton describes his day in the presence of the birds and the books that surround him. There is Vallejo, Rilke, René Char, Montale, Zukofsky, Ungaretti, Edwin Muir, Quasimodo, some Greeks, Nicanor Parra, Chuang Tsu. "Here is the reassuring companionship of many silent Tzu's and Fu's. Kung Tzu, Lao Tzu, Meng Tzu, Tu Fu. And Jui Neng. And Chao-Chu." There are the drawings of Sengai, a scroll from Suzuki. And the sounds of "an Algerian cenobite called Camus," "the clanging prose of Tertullian," "the dry catarrh of Sartre," "the voluble dissonances of Auden," "the golden sounds of John of Salisbury." The "angry birds, Isaias and Jeremias" are there, together with the feminine voices of Angela of Foligno, Flannery O'Connor, Teresa of Avila, Juliana of Norwich, Raissa Maritain. "No lack of voices." Nor does Merton live in a "hermitage," only a house. "What I wear is pants. What I do is live. How I pray is breathe. Who said Zen? Wash out your mouth if you said Zen."[3]

Merton describes his rituals of rising in the night, praying: "the psalms grow up silently by themselves without effort like plants" in a good light. They suspend themselves on "stems of a single consistency—mercy." Their words of sin and redemption, words of blood and anger, are matched by the violence and greed (the nuclear waste and the gold buried at Fort Knox) at the heart of the nation. The ikons of the Holy Virgin remind him of women and marriage (and perhaps his own experience of falling in love, of being loved.) And they remind him of his own final choice of solitude.

> One might say I had decided to marry the silence of the forest. The sweet dark warmth of the whole world will have to be my wife. Out of the heart of that dark warmth comes the secret that is heard only in silence, but is at the root of all the secrets that are whispered by all the lovers in their beds all over world. So perhaps I have an obligation to preserve the stillness, the silence, the poverty, the virginal point of pure nothingness which is the center of all other loves.[4]

There are other rituals—washing the coffee pot, approaching the outhouse with caution because of the king snake who often rests there, spraying for bugs, opening windows, drawing shades against the sun. And there is walking to the monastery and assuming a monk's identity while teaching the novices, who hear "some other person" speaking, before he returns to the woods where he is "nobody."[5]

The non-identity which Merton has long sought is momentarily achieved in a contemplation that is not quite expressible:

> I sit in the cool back room, where words cease to resound, where all meanings are absorbed in the *consonantia* of heat, fragrant pine, quiet wind, bird song, and one central tonic note that is unheard and unuttered. This is no longer a time of obligations. In the silence of the afternoon all is present and all is inscrutable in one central tonic note to which every other sound ascends or descends, to which every other meaning aspires, in order to find its true fulfillment. To ask when the note will sound is to lose the afternoon: it has already sounded, and all things now hum with the resonance of its sounding.[6]

Autobiographically, the point of solitude for Merton, the point of being nobody, of being a stranger, is perhaps this stillness of wordless prayer, a "loss of self" in a union beyond all categories. "Is it true that you are practicing Zen in secret?—Pardon me, I don't speak English."[7]

One can suggest that Merton's own religious and spiritual journey was one in which he was most himself when his life and his writing were in touch with experience, as in this passage. His earlier work was most successful when he himself wrote from experience; he was less successful when he attempted to write theology in the more technical sense, as in *The Ascent to Truth,* or when he attempted to write a kind of traditional piety as in his biographies of Cistercian saints. Even his discussions of the self in *The Silent Life,* in comparison with his later writing and in his own later judgment, are somewhat detached and cerebral, removed from ordinary experience.

The study and practice of Zen, as the art of "seeing into one's own nature," in the words attributed to Bodhidharma, or as a way from bondage to freedom, meant for Merton a new context in which to understand his own monastic and solitary vocation, not as a separation from the world but as a "oneness with all that is."[8] Zen teaching also brought together for him the question of the self and the meaning of wisdom in a way that struck an important chord. For Merton found himself drawn, in all the traditions of wisdom he studied—Eastern Christianity, Russian mysticism, Orthodox Christianity, Islam, Hinduism, Chinese religions, even the Shakers of his own Kentucky—to that deeper knowledge born of the personal realization of wisdom, the experience of ultimate reality, however it is named. Christian mysticism calls it the experience of the presence of God.

Among the sources of Asian wisdom that Merton studied, none attracted him more than Buddhism, especially Zen. His well-known translations of and commentary on the Taoist Chinese sage Chuang Tzu were the result of several years' meditation which persuaded Merton that it was the thought and culture of Chuang Tzu which "transformed highly speculative Indian Buddhism into the humorous, iconoclastic and totally practical kind" of Buddhism that later flourished in the Chinese and Japanese schools of Zen. Merton was drawn by Chuang Tzu as to one who was not interested in formulas and abstractions about reality "but with the direct, existential grasp of reality itself." Chuang Tzu's teaching avoided self-conscious cultivation of the good and fostered rather "the humility of a simple, ordinary life," the "cosmic humility of the man who fully realizes his own nothingness and becomes totally forgetful of himself. . . . " In this there is a psychological analogy, Merton thinks, with the Christian life of faith. And just as Zen illuminates Chuang Tzu, and Chuang Tzu illuminates Zen, so might Zen cast light on the psychology and experience of the self-emptying which unites the Christian with "Christ in His kenosis."[9] And indeed, a new humor and iconoclasm infects Merton's later writing. He clearly succeeds in his goal of not taking himself too seriously!

And it is the relationship of Zen to Christianity that is one of the central issues in the next text to be examined in detail, *Zen and the Birds of Appetite*. The title of the book suggests its central theme: the wisdom Zen might offer to the voracious appetites of Western consciousness, greed, competition, and striving. Merton insists on the vast doctrinal differences between Buddhism and Christianity; they are "worlds apart" theologically, and one must avoid confusing the Christian understanding of the "vision of God" with Buddhist "enlightenment." It is, Merton believes, a mistaken kind of concordist thought which sees too facilely that all mystics experience essentially the same thing, that all religions "meet at the top." Nevertheless, he claims, it is reasonable to compare the *experience* of certain Christian and Buddhist mystics, especially if one is aware "that in certain religions, Buddhism, for instance, the philosophical or religious framework is of a kind that *can* be more easily discarded. . . . " It is not at all clear that this is the case for Christianity. But it is possible to distinguish the "objective theology of Christian experience and the actual psychological facts of Christian mysticism in certain cases." And because Zen is not theology, ideology, or a worldview, it is possible that both Christians and Buddhists can practice it in "the quest for direct and pure experience on a metaphysical level, liberated from verbal formulas and linguistic preconceptions."[10] Merton himself appropriated Zen in this way, in the search for direct experience.

In *Zen and the Birds of Appetite,* Merton writes that objective doctrine is prior in time and importance for Christianity, while experience is always of prior importance in Zen. Because Christianity is founded on a supernatural revelation and is a religion of grace, it is entirely dependent on God. Zen, on the other hand, discards any notion of revelation, "seeks to penetrate the natural ontological ground of being," and "is not easily classified as a religion. . . . " Rather than a message, Zen communicates an awareness that is potentially present in everyone, a universal possibility of consciousness and realization. Thus Zen and Christianity are not incompatible, and Merton finds their special point of complementarity in the question of the self.[11]

Merton describes Zen as teaching nothing. Anyone who claimed to have an authoritative Zen teaching would only have a doctrine about something else, a teaching *about* enlightenment, offering knowledge about an individual understanding but not awakening others to the "Zen in themselves." Zen does not tolerate this sort of imposition. Its purpose is the awakening of a wisdom-intuition *(Prajna)*, an ontological awareness. And such consciousness would not be pure if the one awakened were aware of understanding *Prajna*. Thus Merton says that the language of Zen is a kind of anti-language, and its logic is a reversal of ordinary logic. One can see this anti-language and anti-logic in some of Merton's later writing, and also in his poetry and letters to close friends.

> Zen uses language against itself to blast out . . . preconceptions and to destroy the specious "reality" in our minds so that we can *see directly.* Zen is saying, as Wittgenstein said, "Don't think: Look!"[12]

At the same time, Merton acknowledges that the Zen intuition is "poles apart" from the rationality of linguistic analysis. For Zen attempts to awaken a consciousness that is "beyond the empirical, reflecting, willing and talking ego," a consciousness which is "immediately present to itself and not mediated by either conceptual or reflexive or imaginative knowledge." Merton quotes Suzuki on the series of negations which Zen proposes in the effort to grasp "a plain fact, a pure experience," beyond affirmation and negation. The words and actions of the Zen masters are like an alarm clock awakening a sleeper, rather than signs and symbols pointing to something else.[13]

All this, for Merton, is in sharp contrast to the "stubborn ego-centered practicality" of the West, where everything is ordered to something else, cause to effect, first to next to last without pause. The Zen "fact" is precisely aimed to frustrate this kind of mind, which allows nothing "to be and to mean itself." It does this by intensifying awareness of one's inability to make progress through reasoning or choice. Many Zen stories concern this failure to stop trying to "understand" when one ought simply to look. The enigmatic sayings in these stories must be seen in the context of Buddhist "mindfulness," which sees without interpretation, judgment, or conclusion. Zen aims toward "pure act, pure experience" in an immediacy beyond or prior to the division of subject and object. If one were to try to spell out such immediacy in a philosophical or doctrinal interpretation, for example, as a pantheistic awareness of the Absolute, one has missed the point. One has mistakenly thought Zen to be teaching something when it "explains nothing. It just sees. Sees what? Not an Absolute Object but Absolute Seeing."[14]

Like Christianity, all Buddhism understands ordinary human existence with its confusion and suffering as the ground for a radical transformation of consciousness. But both Buddhism and Christianity go beyond mere explanation of suffering as a problem somehow to be brought under human control.

> Suffering, as both Christianity and Buddhism see, . . . is part of our very ego-identity and empirical existence, and the only thing to do about it is to plunge right into the middle of contradiction and confusion in order to be transformed by what Zen calls the "Great Death" and Christianity calls "dying and rising with Christ."[15]

It is further possible to see the compatibility, especially of the Zen tradition in Buddhism, with Christianity, in light of the importance of direct experience in the Bible, especially the New Testament "word of the Cross." Merton recalls the distinction St. Paul makes (I Cor. 1–2) between two kinds of wisdom, one rational and the other "a matter of paradox and of experience" beyond ordinary reason. Spiritual wisdom is attained when one is liberated from the "wisdom of speech" through the word of the Cross, which confounds both Greeks (philosophy) and Jews (the law). The cross becomes power to those who are freed from legal formulas and conceptual reasoning. One who accepts the "foolishness of God" and "foolish instruments" experiences the "secret and mysterious power" of Christ within as the source of new life and new being.[16]

For Christians, this is no mere theory, but the "stark and existential experience of union with Christ." It means the death of the ego-self as the deepest principle of one's actions and the presence of Christ as their living source. "I live, now not I, but Christ lives in me," Merton repeats, in a new understanding of his favorite words of Paul. The reception of the word of the Cross is an obedient self-emptying in union with Christ. Moving from the level of experience to the level of doctrine about experience, Merton suggests that there is an important analogy between Buddhist *Prajna* as "having the Buddha mind" and the Christian's "having the mind of Christ."[17]

Merton finds a good example of the true Zen experience in the Christian tradition in Meister Eckhart, the fourteenth-century Dominican Rhineland mystic. In an earlier discussion with D. T. Suzuki, Merton had used Cassian's understanding of "purity of heart" as his point of comparison. Now he finds this to have been an unfortunate choice, precisely because purity of heart suggests a place, a pure heart, where God can enter. In *Zen and the Birds of Appetite* he turns to the more paradoxical, extreme, and less orthodox writing of Meister Eckhart, some of whose works had been officially condemned by the church. Merton finds in the Zen descriptions a way of explaining the apparent excesses of Eckhart's mystical expression. And he finds in Eckhart a Christian figure whose experience of the transcendence of self is truly Zen-like.

Not only does Eckhart say that one should "be free from all things and actions" in order to be a dwelling place for God, but that one "should be so poor" that one no longer has "a place for God to act in," so poor that one no longer knows how God is acting within. In Eckhart Merton finds a "Zen-like equation of God as infinite abyss and ground with the true being of the self grounded in [God]." For "only when God acts purely in Himself, do we at last recover our 'true self' (which in Zen terms is 'no-self')."[18]

The poetic rhetoric and baffling illogic in Eckhart's words point to an experience of almost perfect unity, even an *identity,* of the soul with God, which is the divine likeness at the center of one's own being. While Eckhart acknowledges the theological distinction between the Creator and the creature, according to Merton, he also affirms "a basic unity *within* ourselves at the summit of our being where we are 'one with God.' " Merton suggests that one who really reaches this summit would experience the self in an entirely new way and within this unity would know paradoxically both the dignity and the nothingness of the self, would know even the importance of the "earthly self." He finds in Eckhart's mystical description something very close to the Zen masters, yet purely Christian. The pure poverty of one who is no longer a self, who has lost the *persona* that is a separate and special subject even of virtue and the exercises of piety is one who knows the birth of Christ within.[19]

What Merton finds attractive in Eckhart, as in Zen, is the transcendence in the self of the "special, separate cultural and religious identity" that is suggested in both. Even the *persona* that is the subject of virtues and good works is lost, he writes. And this, despite his earlier convictions about the constant necessity of moral reformation, the acquisition of virtue, especially humility, poverty, detachment. And he suggests that this transcendence of the good or moral self is why Eckhart, perhaps deliberately, offended the conventional religious minds of his time.

Merton himself, in these pages and during these years, was struggling toward his own highly autonomous, post-conventional religion. He was seeking a genuine Christian liberty of spirit. A hermit, after all, is very much on his own. And in the talk that Merton later delivered at Bangkok just before his death, he told a story of a Tibetan monk, an abbot who was caught in a critical political situation and who sent a message to another abbot asking what he should do. The message he received was, in Merton's judgment, an important monastic statement: "From now on, everybody stands on his own feet."[20]

This realization of a post-conventional religious autonomy, which includes discovery of the real dignity of the earthly self in the loss of the painful and distracting hyper–self-consciousness of the ego-self, may only be possible for one schooled in the rigorous discipline of a long monastic training, whether Christian or Zen. But Merton does not hesitate to suggest this ultimate possibility for his ordinary Christian readers as an answer to some of the difficult problems of Western consciousness, and as an important focus for interreligious dialogue, especially between Zen and Christianity. But for him the paradox and point of the post-conventional religious autonomy that Zen suggests is finally that of a relativized autonomy. Authentic autonomy, standing on one's own feet, is only reached in the self-loss of religious realization and conversion, the loss of one's illusory autonomy in its claim to absoluteness, in the context of and relationship to the ultimate. This context, Merton continues to maintain, is that of the presence of God.[21]

But what does it really mean to speak of self-loss, no longer to be a self? Merton writes that this kind of mysticism is neither a peak experience, nor a regression into narcissistic tranquility, nor immersion in nature. It is not the self-transcendence of heroic moral courage nor that of aesthetic experience, though these may be concomitant with mystical self-loss. Rather, Merton holds, the transcendent experience of Zen, Sufi, and Christian mysticism

> is an experience of metaphysical or mystical self-transcending [which is] also at the same time an experience of the "Transcendent" or the "Absolute" or "God" not so much as object but Subject.[22]

The Absolute is realized from within itself as well as from within the person, "though 'myself' is now lost and 'found' in God." In Christian terms, the self is at once "metaphysically distinct from God and yet perfectly identified with that Self by love and freedom, so that there appears to be but one Self." Transcendent experience in this sense is "the illumination of wisdom (*Sapientia, Sophia, Prajna*)." In this experience, one somehow enters the reality of things, knows the meaning of one's own transient existence, and relates to all in identity and love. The idea of being "no longer a self," Merton notes, must not be interpreted theologically but rather in terms of the *experience* it is meant to describe.[23]

For Merton, this experience transcends ordinary religious experience or insight in which self-awareness is intensified and purified. Rather, in mystical transcendent experience a revolutionary change occurs such that it is precisely *not* the ego-self or empirical subject who is the recipient of some extraordinary and self-fulfilling experiences. He notes that the mystical traditions unconditionally question the notion of an experience that is analogous to other intense experiences of the limited, conscious subject and affirm that the subject of the experience is no longer conscious of itself as separate and unique. "If the empirical ego is conscious at all, [it is] conscious of itself as transcended, left behind, irrelevant, illusory, and indeed as the root of all ignorance *(Avidya)*." [24]

Merton describes transcendent experience as a kind of "superconsciousness." The Zen "unconscious" is not psychological but metaphysical. The Christian idea of *raptus,* he says, strictly speaking, is neither aesthetic nor erotic experience but an ontological state of being above oneself *(supra se).* The focus of the Zen experience is the Self or Void and not the ego-self. And the focus of the Christian experience is Christ or the Holy Spirit—away from the self yet within the self. Merton notes that the language of the mystics is intended to be taken with careful qualification; yet its point is that "the subject of this transcendent consciousness is not the ego as isolated and contingent, but the person as 'found' and 'actualized' in union with Christ." The Christian tradition of mysticism never designates the empirical ego, and "still less the neurotic and narcissistic self," but always the "person" whose identity is one with Christ. Thus Merton again uses the notion of "person" to indicate the transformation of Christian consciousness which occurs as participation "in the mind of Christ," a kenotic transformation of ego-consciousness that is of such transparency that only identity-language can express it.[25]

In relation to the theme of the self, these discussions in *Zen and the Birds of Appetite* show the different languages which Merton uses to distinguish the various levels of the self or ways to approach the self. First, there is still present the distinction he draws from Maritain between the individual, rooted in matter, and the person, rooted in spirit. It is important to remember, however, that Maritain, following Thomas Aquinas, insisted on the "hylomorphic" unity of matter and spirit in the person. In this unity, according to both Maritain and Merton, if the material pole or the individual dominates, the true spiritual nature of the person is distorted and never fully emerges in personal or societal life. It is this "individual" that Merton variously names as the empirical ego or the exterior or false or external self. In certain circumstances, this self can also be named the illusory self, because it is illusion to judge that the individual or empirical ego is the whole self. When such illusion completely—that is, obsessively or compulsively—takes over the whole self in its general orientation, then there is what Merton, especially during his period of psychological interest, calls the "neurotic" self, a distorted, mere shadow or sham of the person.

At the other, spiritual pole of the matter-spirit unity that is "man" for Merton, there is the created, natural person who is spirit incarnate in matter. This is the "person" who orders the material side of its being according to the knowledge and the love of other persons and of God in authentic Christian sacramentality. In the Christian order, it is the created spiritual person who is made, in fact, for a new creation. In Merton's fundamentally Thomist scheme, this new creation both restores the original contemplative self of creation, lost in original sin, and transforms this natural self in the new life that is the grace of Christ, a participation in God's life.

As Merton looked at Zen, he understood it as helpful to Christians precisely because it was a way to release the dominating hold, so prevalent in the West, of the exterior or illusory self, the individual or the empirical ego, on the whole person. Zen offers a way of releasing the inner, metaphysical, natural self that is the substratum for what Christianity describes as the action of grace or the "birth of Christ" in the person. Merton maintains that Christianity speaks of an entirely new level of personal transformation, the "supernatural." But this transformation cannot be effected unless the inner, natural self is allowed to emerge as the true center of the person.

Thus, in *Zen and the Birds of Appetite,* Merton writes that in Zen there is a pattern not entirely foreign to Christianity in which "the individual ego is completely emptied and becomes identified with the enlightened Buddha, . . . finds itself to be in reality the enlightened Buddha mind." Nirvana, the awakening which is the goal of Buddhist discipline, is not the self-awareness of having crossed to the "other shore," in a common Buddhist metaphor, but an absolute consciousness of the Void "in which there are no shores." The pattern of emptying and enlightenment is similar to Christian kenosis (emptying). The difference is that the Buddhist experience is existential and ontological (the opening out of the inner or metaphysical self of creation) while the Christian experience is theological and personal (the graced awareness of God).[26]

Merton emphasizes that ascetic self-emptying is the way to transcendence in all major religious traditions, and insists that transcendent experience is never merely a means of affirmation or fulfillment of the self. One is not "realized" in one's limited selfhood but simply "disappears." This does not mean the loss of metaphysical identity but that one's "real status is quite other than what appears empirically. . . . " Thus the importance of detachment from the usual conceptions of the self, particularly the idea of oneself as a candidate for realization, and the importance of the ruthless combat in both Christian and Buddhist traditions against spiritual ambition. Traditional spiritual disciplines lead one to relax one's conception of the goal of self-transcendence and especially of "who it is" who attains it.

"To cling too tenaciously to the 'self' and its own fulfillment would guarantee that there would be no fulfillment at all," Merton writes. It is the metaphysical person, not the psychological ego, which is capable of transcendent experience, of authentic "union with the Ground of Being." Hence if one were to attempt to go outside the self to experience the self, the "unitive wisdom experience would become impossible," since one would be split into an observing and an experiencing self. This is the source of "the paradox that as soon as there is 'someone there' to have transcendent experience, the experience is falsified and indeed becomes impossible." The paradox is of an "experience" that transcends mere psychological "experience," an experience which one has and in some way knows, but one does not know it as "one's own."[27]

For Merton, the most important issue at stake in the religious dialogue between East and West is not a matter of substantive theology but a matter of consciousness. Western failure to get beyond such categories as "pantheism" or life-denying "quietism" in approaching the religious thought of Asia is rooted in the anti-mystical bias of Christian consciousness today. In Merton's interpretation, recent historical and biblical theology have entailed a fundamental criticism of the Hellenic and metaphysical orientations which had led Christianity in the Middle Ages to move away from the primitive Christian sense of dynamic, "existential . . . encounter with God in Christ and in the church as a *happening.*" Ancient and medieval interpretations tended to place an emphasis on static *being* as "a new ontological status and a 'new nature.' Grace was understood not as God's act but as the sharing of the divine nature in 'divinization.' " Divinization and being, of course, are fundamental categories for Merton's own mentors, the Eastern fathers of the church and the monastic fathers as well. And they represent the metaphysical basis of the medieval mysticism to which he was so attracted.

Progressive Christians today, Merton writes, tend to reject mystical consciousness (identified with the Hellenic or the medieval) as not really Christian or biblical. And so Merton asks, in this context, whether the long tradition of Christian mysticism, from "the Alexandrian and Cappadocian Fathers, down to Eckhart, Tauler, the Spanish mystics and the modern mystics," is simply an aberration. Again, this is the tradition of Merton's own Christian formation, the tradition that had so drawn him in his early years in the monastery. And thus his questions have a special poignancy: Is biblical and prophetic Christianity fundamentally opposed to mystical Christianity?[28]

The historical issue is further complicated, in Merton's understanding, by the problem of modern consciousness. It is simply impossible for contemporary persons to adopt the mind of first-century Christians. The overwhelming significance of the turn to the subject in modern consciousness, symbolized for Merton by the Cartesian *cogito,* means that the Western individual

> is a subject for whom his own self-awareness as a thinking, observing, measuring and estimating "self" is absolutely primary. It is . . . the one indubitable "reality," and all truth starts here.[29]

In Merton's view, this consciousness develops as one sees oneself as a subject over against objects to be manipulated for one's own interests. This consciousness tends to isolate the self into a detached observer, a "solipsistic bubble of awareness—an ego-self" cut off from other selves. This can lead to the extreme of an objectifying consciousness in which even God eventually becomes an object. And when God is made into an object like other objects of experience, the reality of God "dies." Hence, in addition to the "death of God," modern times have also witnessed the struggle of the self to break loose from itself in "openness" and "encounter," to recover an authentic "I–Thou" relationship. This is an extremely difficult project for a "purely Cartesian subject," that is, a consciousness that has detached itself psychologically from its roots in spirit, its ontological roots in communion with Being and other beings.

There is, however, another metaphysical consciousness available for modern persons, in Merton's judgment. And again, he turns to Maritain's metaphysical understanding of the person, derived from Thomas Aquinas. This consciousness

> starts not from the thinking and self-aware subject but from Being, ontologically seen to be beyond and prior to the subject-object division. Underlying the subjective experience of the individual self there is an immediate experience of Being. This is totally different from the experience of self-consciousness. It is completely non-objective. It has none of the split and alienation that occurs when the subject becomes aware of itself as a quasi-object.[30]

In this statement, one notices the thought pattern that contemporary "transcendental" interpreters of Aquinas—Rahner, for example, use to develop a Thomist theological anthropology precisely on the basis of the modern philosophical "turn to the subject." In this perspective, the experience of the self, in its depth, can be shown to be the experience of God, since the self as subject is dimly aware of God as the horizon or the constant presence that is the source of its own subjectivity.[31]

For Merton, the kind of consciousness suggested by Maritain, whether positively experienced (as an abundance of being) or negatively experienced (as nothingness), transcends reflexive awareness in an immediacy in which there is no longer "consciousness *of* but *pure* consciousness"; the subject as it were disappears. It reemerges, to be sure, beyond the experience of immediacy, but as a self-aware subject which is not final but provisional, now relative to God and to others. It is to this consciousness, Merton believes, that both Asian and Christian mystical traditions witness in their language of "letting go," ecstasy, self-loss in God. In Christian terms, the self is no longer centered on itself but on God, in whom everyone else is present. Hence this consciousness is open to encounter with others from the very beginning. It is ontologically based on an original intuition of the ground of openness which is the ground of being, prior to the subject/object split of Cartesian thought.

It is this consciousness that needs to be recovered, Merton

writes, in *Zen and the Birds of Appetite*. And it can be recovered in nonmystical terms in the encounter with God "not as Being but as Freedom and Love." This gracious and prophetic experience need not be opposed to the metaphysical and the mystical since the two approaches can, from this perspective, be understood as seeking the same consciousness, the same encounter in awareness.

Merton is not, however, entirely hopeful about the prospects for this recovery of contemplative consciousness for Western Christianity. The difficulties are immense despite all the arguments that can be made in its favor.

> It is quite plausible to assert that the old Hellenic categories are indeed worn out, and that Platonizing thought, even revivified with shots in the arm from Yoga and Zen, will not serve in the modern world.[32]

But if any opening is possible for Christian consciousness today, it will have to meet what Merton distinguishes as the four great contemporary Western needs: (1) the need for authentic community, (2) the need for ultimate meaning in ordinary life, (3) the need for an integrated experience of the self in all its dimensions (bodily, imaginative, emotional, intellectual, spiritual), and especially (4) the need for liberation from an extreme of self-consciousness and self-awareness.[33]

In relation to all these needs, and particularly the last, Merton believes that the teaching of Buddhism on "ignorance, deliverance, enlightenment" may be discovered to shed new light on the liberation of which the Christian gospel speaks. And in Merton's own thought, the chief focus of this kind of dialogue between traditions might well be the teaching on the self, its real identity, its experience of itself and the importance of self-loss in the finding, the recovery of the true self. The Buddhist traditions, and especially Zen, may offer a wisdom for which there is desperate need in the West.[34]

Merton finds in the study and practice of Zen a teaching that illuminates his own deepest Christian intuitions, especially about the nature of the experience of the self. For he experienced the self as a source of both deception and of truth in his own spiritual search. In fact, our study of the theme of the self in his thought shows that he began, in his earliest spiritual writing, with his own experience. When Merton moves away from experience and attempts to write a more structured, "doctrinal" kind of work, as in *The Silent Life,* his work becomes less immediate, more detached, less engaging. In *Zen and the Birds of Appetite,* he is once more in touch with experience and the questions his own experience raises with regard to the problem of the self. Paradoxically, it is the issue of self-forgetfulness—the renunciation of experience and of the search for extraordinary experience—that enables Merton to integrate his religious and psychological insights on the question of the self.

In relation to the central needs which he sees in the West — personal community, meaning in ordinary life, integration of fragmented experience, liberation from exaggerated self-awareness—Merton translates the goal of simplicity and wisdom witnessed in the contemplative traditions of East and West into contemporary language. It is "cosmic humility," the consequence of the immediacy of mystical experience, of "seeing," that is the analogous goal of Christian contemplation and Zen meditation and that might offer wisdom to the contemporary world, especially the West, with its voracious "appetites." For both traditions, the death of the ego-self is the psychological counterpart to metaphysical awakening. In Christian terms, the pattern of the cross and resurrection means a transformation of consciousness from the self-interested, everyday ego-self or individual to the selfless person united with God in Christ. The goal of such transformation, generally lost in the excessive self-consciousness of the West may, in Merton's judgment, be recovered through dialogue with Eastern traditions, a dialogue centered not so much on the content of doctrines or theology as on the issue of consciousness, experience, and the meaning of the self.

Merton's approach to Asian religions, as exemplified in his treatment of Zen in *Zen and the Birds of Appetite,* combines a thoroughly Christian perspective with a thoroughly open and uninhibited approach to the world of Zen experience. Although as a Christian, Merton is led to make comparisons, there are no "cheap" contrasts in his assessment of relationships. Rather, his comparisons are searching ones, illuminating, respectful, irenic. While he espoused no technical theological or philosophical theory of the religions, his life and thought embody the ideal of dialogue: a willingness to learn from the other and to communicate with the other without surrendering one's own point of view. The fruit of Merton's dialogue with the other, in this case with Zen, lies in an enrichment of his own experience, understanding and writing.

Yet Merton is himself a Christian and remains Christian throughout his exploration of Asian traditions. His personal assimilation of Zen, like his extensive reading and his absorption in other forms of Eastern thought during his Asian travels in the last months of his life, enriched but did not radically alter his thoroughly Christian identity. For he was interested in the teachings or doctrines of the other traditions as a way to understand the religious, and especially the mystical or contemplative, *experience* of persons of other traditions and the wisdom their experience might offer.

And Merton's identity as a monk does not change. He is deeply concerned with his own monastic tradition and with learning from the other monastic worlds he encountered as he met with other monks and holy men, both Buddhist and Christian. He is happy to identify himself simply as a tourist on his travels, wears his Cistercian habit when he meets the Dalai Lama, and has some of his most memorable Asian encounters with several *rimpoches* who, like himself, had spent many years in meditation and who recognize in him a genuine brother, a fellow searcher. Merton's search, however open to the thought worlds and the categories of other traditions, was that of a monk who remained convinced that the monastic *experience* had something important to offer the ordinary readers in the West for whom he wrote.

And it is the experience of a very contemporary, religiously and intellectually sophisticated *Christian* monk that is communicated in his last books, where the theme of the self continues to be a central issue.

5

"I LIVE NOW NOT I . . ."

The two final texts in which Merton focuses explicitly on the theme of the self are *Contemplation in a World of Action* (1971) and *Contemplative Prayer* (1969). Both books were published after Merton's tragic death in December of 1968, from manuscripts he had already finished.

The two texts represent very different sides of Merton the monk. *Contemplation in a World of Action* reflects the more practical side of Merton's thought during his final years. It reveals a man who is deeply involved in directing novices and young monks and in the question of renewal as it relates to the monastic life in the turbulent years following the Second Vatican Council. *Contemplative Prayer* shows the Merton who has immersed himself in study of the theology of the church fathers, the desert and monastic fathers, especially St. Benedict and the Benedictine tradition as it developed in the Middle Ages, and the mystical tradition, including especially John of the Cross and the fourteenth-century Rhineland figures, Tauler, Ruysbroeck, and Eckhart. *Contemplative Prayer* represents Merton's own tradition of monastic contemplation, newly interpreted in the light of existentialist philosophy, while *Contemplation in a World of Action* reflects his attempt to relate that tradition to the vicissitudes of church renewal in the contemporary world, especially contemporary experience as it is understood in psychological terms.

Merton himself, in his final years, embodied the struggle between tradition and "modernity." As we have already noted, after his many discussions of the importance of solitude and his arguments from tradition for the hermit's life as the natural outgrowth of years in the discipline of the communal monastic setting, Merton finally obtained permission to live alone in a hermitage on the grounds at Gethsemani. But his biographers have revealed that his hermitage was the scene not only of solitude but of many visits from friends outside the monastery. And, to the surprise and consternation of his superiors, Merton began to talk about plans for travel. He wanted to search for a setting that would provide him greater solitude, perhaps in California or Alaska, and he wanted to make personal contact with both Asian Christian monks and with monks and religious seekers of other religious traditions in Asia.

Merton's final journey to the East, movingly recorded in *The Asian Journal*, describes him as a very happy traveler who hoped to resolve his own great question in the course of his journey to India, Thailand, and Ceylon, with extended stops beforehand in California and Alaska. *The Asian Journal* reveals his deeply sympathetic meetings with various holy men in India and Thailand, his "breakthrough" experience when he viewed the statues at Polonnaruwa in Ceylon (now Sri Lanka), and his hopes for further travel in the future, at least to Japan and to Scotland in search for a place of hermitage which would allow him greater solitude, and perhaps to Greece to visit a friend from his Columbia days. Nevertheless, he is clear that he is and will remain a monk of Gethsemani wherever he decides to settle in the future. Merton's accidental death by electrocution occurred in Bangkok, where he was attending a meeting of the monks of Asia, just after he had addressed the conference on "Marxism and Monastic Perspectives." At the end of his talk, he casually remarked, after indicating the schedule for meeting again later in the evening, "So I will disappear."[1]

While the two texts, *Contemplation in a World of Action* and *Contemplative Prayer*, represent something of a paradox in demonstrating the intensely spiritual and solidly practical sides of Merton's thought on the question of the self, together they reveal the complex depth of that thought and suggest ways that the attentive interpreter may finally draw its various strands into a unified whole. These texts also can symbolize the dimensions of Merton's own final spiritual journey from the false to the true self and from monastic asceticism and discipline to the spiritual liberation that is the goal of the monastic life. For Merton it was a journey from the artificiality of an external identity imposed by his *persona* either as monk or writer to the true self of the person who realizes in experience a relationship to all others, even others of radically distant times and places, in relationship to the ultimate reality that is God.

Since the practical foundations of Merton's full thought on the question of the self are worked out most carefully in some of the essays in *Contemplation in a World of Action,* we first turn to that book in which Merton ruminates on the problems of monastic renewal following Vatican Council II and its directives for *aggiornamento.* The central problem, as Merton sees it, is to adapt old structures and patterns in a way that does not lose, but in fact deepens, awareness of the heart and purpose of the monastic life. That heart and purpose is the call to experience the presence of God in silence and solitude, the call to a life of contemplation which is an experience of transformation in Christ. Merton deals especially with the importance of dialogue in the process of renewal—dialogue with modern thought as it implicitly shapes and forms the personalities of those who come to the monasteries of the modern world, dialogue with the various movements of American culture, and dialogue within the global context which is the new environment of both Catholicism and monasticism since the Second Vatican Council.

The focus of Merton's discussions of the self in this framework is the character and formation of the young Americans who seek to become monks today. He writes, in an essay on "The Identity Crisis," about the widespread crisis of religious vocations: both the departure of so many who had apparently been good monks and the difficulties of new monks in adopting the traditional monastic discipline. He refers to modern thinkers, Marx, Darwin, Kierkegaard, Freud, Jung, Sartre, and others, as secular prophets who have described the contemporary world by pointing out that people today are not themselves. They have lost themselves "in the falsities and illusions of a massive organization." Thus the young people who come to the monastery now seek not only authentic human and religious values in contrast to the requirements of an ancient code of laws but are also in the throes of a psychological identity crisis that they hope to work out in the monastic setting.

> One of the characteristics of "mass society" is precisely that it tends to keep [one] from fully achieving [one's] identity, from operating fully as an autonomous person, from growing up and becoming spiritually and emotionally adult.[2]

By identity, in this passage, Merton means having one's own genuine and personal beliefs and convictions as these are based on one's own developed experience of oneself as a person. It is the "experience of one's ability to choose or reject even good things which are not relevant to one's own life." Thus Merton refers to the natural self and its development of a basic psychological autonomy.

In this sense, he writes, one is not simply given an identity with one's birth but must struggle to create an identity for oneself by significant choices that demand risk and courage. This personal identity is the reality of a deep and centered self, which then knows its own experience and can reflect and judge according to its own values. And it is this sense of natural, human identity that is a precondition for any responsible and adult spiritual choice in relation to God and to others, especially the choice of monastic life as a response to God's call. Merton's conviction about the importance of this psychological, adult identity comes from his own experience in working with the postulants and novices at Gethsemani. He fears that too often the monastery and its discipline can serve as a refuge for those who are unable or

unwilling to face themselves and who merely attempt to evade
authentic personal decision by looking for security in pleasing
authority, allowing someone or something else to establish right
and wrong for them. "This passive and evasive response to the
identity problem is a false solution," he writes.[3]

Another problem is that sometimes the more mature novice is
scandalized because he sees older monks who have settled for an
inauthentic routine existence in the security of the monastery.
Some of these older monks may be known as "characters" or "ec-
centrics" in the monastery and the new members fear that they
will become like these less than exemplary spiritual models. Unwilling to make that "sacrifice" of themselves for an external
ideal, they leave because they know something more is required
of them than mere submission to an external control. And at the
very basic, human level they are right in their judgment that this
kind of evasion of personal responsibility is false. Merton writes:

> To renounce one's autonomy to the point of abandoning all sponta-
> neous and independent reflection, intellection, volition, even feel-
> ing, is sometimes presented as an ascetic ideal. But this is an
> impossibility, and even the idea that such a thing is desirable can
> do irreparable harm. The attempt to live in this manner and to
> make others do so, is gravely damaging to souls and is a flagrant
> violation of Christian truth and of the integrity of the human person
> made in God's image. Our monastic life can at times suffer seriously
> from this overcontrol.[4]

In these remarks, one senses that Merton himself may have
suffered, toward the end of his life, from "overcontrol," from interpretations of monastic discipline that simply encouraged a
false kind of imitation of pious roles. But he may also have discovered that his own earlier writings about the self may have
presumed too much about the kind of persons formed in the
modern societal context. Before one is ready for the asceticism
and deeply spiritual "loss of self" about which he had written so
enthusiastically and eloquently, one must have a self, the fully
developed self that Merton himself was when he came to Chris-

tianity and to the monastery. Now the difficult task of working
with very young Americans, often teenagers and "television ad-
dicts," has taught him some important psychological lessons
about the needs of adolescent and adult development on the natural plane before the austere demands of the spiritual life can be
met and embraced.

As Merton theorizes about the problem of identity, he suggests that systemization of control is one of the general and
central problems of Western secular life, especially under the influence of the mass media, just as much as it is in the rigidly
controlled totalitarian societies of the communist nations. The
control in the West is simply more anonymous, where the con-
sumer, for example, is "treated consistently as a minor and maintained in a state of psychological passivity and dependence." In
sum, the modern person is alienated, "systematically deprived of
a serious identity." And the alienated person, who exists for
something or somebody else, has nothing to give and so cannot
love. "The lover is able to give himself completely to another
precisely because he is his own to give."[5]

Without this kind of self-possession, a spirituality of self-loss
will seem to require the sacrifice of personal authenticity and integrity, Merton realizes. Notions of obedience and humility will
seem to require "the complete abdication of one's personal autonomy and dignity" and obedience will become mere passive
compliance, a lack of adult responsibility. Theologically, Merton
points out that a "spirituality which despises nature and con-
temns the human person is basically divisive and Manichean,"
and implies a dualistic concept of God and creation in which
creation is seen as opposed or alien to God, "cursed rather than
blessed and redeemed." By the incarnation and redemption,
Merton writes, nature has been transformed by grace. Nature,
to use an image from his earlier *Seeds of Contemplation,* is the
ground in which the seed of grace is planted. And the nature of
the self must be respected and developed before the grace of self-
giving or self-loss can have effect.

In Merton's view, the solitary character of monastic life can

be distorted to mean simply a secure existence in which the
monk may fail to achieve or even strive for identity and authenticity. However, he insists, "it is not for us to surrender our monastic life and its tradition, but to get down to its real meaning
and revive its genuine values." This will mean, he speculates, a
new kind of education that prepares the natural, human person
for monastic culture. This education should include, most importantly, an appropriate balance of contact with contemporary
life and the reappropriation of good, cooperative manual work
in nature itself, in order that the modern monk may move toward that "final integration" which is the goal of monastic life.[6]

"Final Integration" is the title of the second essay in *Contemplation in a World of Action* that is relevant to the theme of the
self. It is subtitled "Toward a Monastic Therapy" and reflects
Merton's continuing interest in psychology and its relation to the
experience of the spiritual life. Merton's concern in this essay is
that the point of monastic life, a genuine "rebirth" or "transformation" in Christ, is often forgotten as practical issues of
efficiency and good order dominate discussion of renewal. He is
dubious, in this context, about the use of American psychotherapy, which, he fears, counsels only "adjustment to reality" and
thus leads to a kind of mediocrity in the very people whose goal
is an exploration of the depths of both human and religious possibility. Authentic "rebirth" and "transformation" are central to
the traditional idea of monastic *conversatio,* or the vow of *conversio morum* (for Merton, the most "mysterious" of the monastic
vows). But in fact few experience the monastic discipline as really
helping them to find their way toward their original deepest as-
pirations to radical transformation. Merton writes:

> The notion of "rebirth" is not peculiar to Christianity. In Sufism,
> Zen Buddhism and in many other religious or spiritual traditions,
> emphasis is placed on the call to fulfill certain obscure yet urgent
> potentialities in the ground of one's being, to "become someone"
> that one already (potentially) is, the person one is truly meant to

be. Zen calls this awakening a recognition of "your original face before you were born."[7]

But, Merton questions, how many spiritual seekers really reach the transcultural goal of transformation common to these traditions?

In all the traditions, the importance of an experienced guide or a spiritual director in this quest is stressed. In the monastic setting, where the guide is less central, vibrant and spirit-filled liturgical celebration might compensate for direct guidance but often in contemporary monasteries and liturgies there is no sense of "the urgency of inner development" and little aspiration to authentic "rebirth." When this is the case, something very important is missing which is not made up for by regular practice of public worship and careful observance of the rules of enclosure which keep the monks from all contact with the world. In fact, this situation can lead simply to an impoverishment and a stifling of the personality.

Merton turns to the work of a Persian psychoanalyst who practices in America (Reza Arasteh) and who uses insights from humanistic psychology (Erich Fromm and Viktor Frankl), as well as the mystical theories of Sufism to explore "the final and complete maturing of the human psyche on a transcultural level." Transcultural maturity is something beyond mere cure of neurosis or adaptation to society. This point is especially important, Merton believes, if one's society is as unhealthy as American society is, with "its overemphasis on cerebral, competitive, acquisitive forms of ego-affirmation," and so inhibits genuine spiritual growth. He argues that American psychiatry often becomes a "technique for making people conform to a society that prevents them from growing and developing as they should," precisely by encouraging the troubled or questioning individual to follow the herd values of the crowd rather than promoting "creative dissent" and efforts to change society in more humane directions.[8]

Merton's own social criticism on the issues of race, violence, war and peace, his dissent from American policies on nuclear buildup and from the earlier position of the American Catholic hierarchy on the Viet Nam War are recalled when he comments that psychotherapy has been put in the service of a society that is a "massive, affluent organization." This is a society that is supposedly dedicated to freedom and yet tolerates less and less dissent.

Merton distinguishes, following Arasteh, "mere neurotic anxiety" from "existential anxiety." The former is a petulant, self-defeating sorrow; the latter is a call to growth and is a sign of health. For it is the beginning of a possible movement toward psychic rebirth into a new identity which transcends the limits of societal and religious conventions. And it is "an imperative necessity" in order that one be drawn out of one's original narcissism and self-centeredness toward a new identity as a socially responsible member of society. Beyond this there is a further rebirth, the "final integration," the authentic goal which draws one to a monastery or to a deeper life of prayer. In traditional religious terms, final integration can be named holiness or sanctity.

> Final integration is a state of transcultural maturity far beyond mere social adjustment, which always implies partiality and compromise. [One] who is "fully born" has an entirely different inner experience of life." [One] apprehends [one's] life fully and wholly from an inner ground that is at once more universal than the empirical ego and yet entirely [one's] own. [One] is in a certain sense "cosmic" and "universal. . . . " [One] has attained a deeper, fuller identity than that of [the] limited ego-self which is only a fragment of [one's] being. [One] is in a certain sense identified with everybody: or in the familiar language of the New Testament . . . "all things to all [people]."[9]

Merton describes this integration as one in which the person has a deep, inner freedom that allows her or him to experience the feelings of others without being dominated by them, a freedom that is spontaneous and dynamic. This freedom reminds him of St. Thomas Aquinas, who teaches that the gifts of the Holy Spirit enable one to live and to act "in a superhuman mode." This new state includes the openness, emptiness, and poverty described by the Christian mystics, by the Sufis, the Taoist masters, and Zen Buddhists, attitudes which point to docility to the Spirit and to a potency for an authentic creativity that is universal, not limited by the person's own culture. One is a "fully comprehensive 'self' " who has unified the diversity of cultures in a personal and dialectical kind of insight and so can bring "perspective, liberty and spontaneity" into the lives of others. This full self is a peacemaker—and hence the urgent need for national and world leaders who are fully born, mature persons. And such persons are the kind that monastic life ideally should produce.[10]

When Merton writes about liberty of spirit—"liberation from the limits of all that is merely partial and fragmentary in a given culture"—we are able to understand some of the paradoxical elements in his own life during his last years: his search for greater personal solitude and his travels and intensified contacts with other people, his affirmation of the disciplines of the ancient monastic tradition and his own freedom in breaking the rules, his continued allegiance to Christianity and his experiential participation in other religions. He cites no less an authority than St. Benedict, who speaks of a "new identity, the new mode of being of the monk who no longer practices the various degrees of humility" in studied fashion but rather with "dynamic spontaneity 'in the Spirit.' " Merton suggests that if whole communities were to reach such final integration the effect would indeed be revolutionary. And he realizes that there is often an unconscious attempt in monastic and church communities to keep things under control, even the Holy Spirit! And yet monastic life is meant to be charismatic. Too much control leads to "a prevalence of neurosis, of masochism, of obsessions and compulsions, of fanaticism, intolerance, narrow-mindedness, and various petty forms of de-

structive cruelty. . . . " One senses in these comments a bit of
disillusionment and frustration in Merton's perception of the
contrast between the monastic ideal and his real life experience.[11]

But disillusionment and frustration never have the last word
with Merton. He digs more deeply and observes that the rebirth
that precedes final integration entails an extreme crisis, a dark
night, what the Sufis call *Fana,* an annihilation or disintegration,
a self-loss or spiritual death. This is followed, however, by *Baqa*
or reintegration. And the whole process involves an anguished
interior solitude, an "existential moratorium," and a "courage
that is related to the root of all existence." This anguish cannot
be "cured" but only lived through: none of the familiar props of
ordinary family or societal life suffice as one becomes, in Jungian
terms, "individuated," or removed "from the undifferentiated
and unconscious herd," in a favorite Merton phrase of these last
years.[12]

Merton worries that this solitary, personal adventure is almost
too hazardous, too risky, too disturbing for any ordinary monastery to embrace. And yet he suspects that the price monastic
life will pay for not encouraging such liberty of spirit is frustration and mediocrity. Hence he maintains that the monastic renewal ought to bring about the development of structures that
encourage this rebirth and transformation for *everybody* because,
beyond the psychological level, a Christian transcultural integration is an eschatological aim that is theologically required.

> The rebirth of man and of society on a transcultural level is a rebirth
> into the transformed and redeemed time, the time of the Kingdom,
> the time of the Spirit, the time of "the end." It means a disin-
> tegration of the social and cultural self, the product of merely hu-
> man history, and the reintegration of that self in Christ, in salvation
> history, in the mystery of redemption, in the Pentecostal "new cre-
> ation." But this means entering into the full mystery of the escha-
> tological Church.[13]

The important fact about final integration for today, Merton suggests, is that it is becoming a need and a hope not just for monks and other religious specialists but for everyone. The whole world is in a state of crisis and the solutions which are generally offered are either tragic—as military, economic, and political resources are marshalled to block real change and maintain established patterns of profit—or foolishly optimistic: "a kind of hippie kingdom of love in a cybernated and peace-loving mega-city (presumably with free LSD for everybody)." And Christians line up on both sides here, Merton notes, although probably the majority mistakenly believe that Christ is identified with Western capitalism.[14]

Merton believes that neither choice is really Christian. The true solution lies in the Spirit who will speak at the right moment through a renewed church and monastic community. Integration for the individual and the community, he concludes, lies outside the agendas of culture, including even "Christian culture." Merton's own "transcultural integration," if an interpretative guess may be hazarded, goes beyond the Christian and monastic culture of his own spiritual formation to include, within his own dialectical perspective, something of the spiritual experience of many cultures: Russian and Greek Orthodoxy, the Sufis of Islam, Asian Hinduism, Buddhism, Zen, Taoism, Confucianism, the Shakers of his own adopted Kentucky. The experience of any religious group or person which cherishes the solitary personal search for rebirth and transformation attracts Merton's transcultural mind and spirit. And yet he never left the particularity of his own Christian, Catholic, and monastic religious heritage. In that particularity Merton sought to uncover something universal.

Thus it is no surprise that his final book, *Contemplative Prayer* (or as it is titled in another edition, *The Climate of Monastic Prayer),* and his final text on the theme of the self is one in which he returns to the monastic and mystical tradition.[15] The specific problem Merton addresses in this final text on contemplation is the relation between the liturgy as the formal, official prayer of the church (especially the hours of the Divine Office sung by the monks in choir) and contemplative or personal prayer. And he deals with the issue by probing the understanding of prayer found in the Bible and the writings of the desert and monastic fathers and the mystics of the Christian tradition. In the course of his explorations, Merton returns to his own theology of the false and true self, but now at a new depth, that of the radical self-questioning that he calls "existential dread" or "monastic dread." His reading of the existentialist philosophers, especially Kierkegaard, Heidegger, and Sartre, is apparent in his choice of the word "dread" to name the radical experience of abandoning the false self, the role which each of us plays in society. And again, while this book is written primarily for monks, Merton suggests that it is adaptable for all Christians seeking the depths of the life of the spirit.

Merton affirms that monastic prayer, in its primitive context, is essentially simple and nonliturgical. The early monks did not look for extraordinary experiences in their prayer but struggled for the purity of heart which enabled concentration on love and service of God. Their prayer was drawn from Scripture, especially the Psalms. The Psalter revealed for them "the secret movements of the heart in its struggle against the forces of darkness." The first monks memorized the words of the Bible in order to repeat them "from the heart." And "the heart" was understood "as the root and source of one's own inner truth." Merton refers to the *Philokalia,* a handbook of quotations from the Eastern monastic fathers used by the Greek and Russian monks. These are quotations about the "prayer of the heart," or the "prayer of Jesus," which was so important in the hesychastic (quiet) contemplation of the monastic centers of Sinai and Mt. Athos. These sources indicate, for Merton, the essentially simple prayer of early monasticism, a simplicity which can easily be related to contemplation. And he points out that the ancient prayer of the heart can be related as well to modern existentialist thought which emphasizes the human need to face the fact of death, the need for authenticity, and the need for an authentic inner liberation. Thus the climate of inner struggle that is the context of monastic prayer is not totally unlike the climate of the world today, a climate of existential crisis and struggle and a widespread experience of dread.

Merton insists that the way of monastic prayer is not escape from human suffering but rather shares in the ordinary human anguish of self-searching, nausea at one's own vanity, one's "falsity and capacity for betrayal."

> Far from establishing one in unassailable narcissistic security, the way of prayer brings us face to face with the sham and indignity of the false self that seeks to live for itself alone and to enjoy the "consolation of prayer" for its own sake. This "self" is pure illusion, and ultimately [one] who lives for and by such an illusion must end either in disgust or in madness.[16]

Ordinary social life encourages an illusory, narcissistic existence, Merton says. Human alienation and confusion in modern society are even made to seem bearable because they are such common experiences. But eventually the "ground of doubt and self-questioning under all life brings one to face questions of ultimate meaning." And this self-questioning brings with it "existential dread," an insecurity, lostness, exile, sin, a sense that one has not been true to "one's inmost truth."

> "Dread" in this sense is not simply a childish fear of retribution, or a naive guilt, a fear of violating taboos. It is the profound awareness that one is capable of ultimate bad faith with [one]self and with others: that one is living a lie.[17]

In the monastic setting, this radical self-questioning includes awareness that most organizational life and its "approved way" may themselves promote this falseness and illusion. Thus "monastic dread" is the interior struggle over whether fidelity to God and to self is calling one to break out of familiar and established routines, to leave the security of rules, and to move into the unknown. Monastic dread can also be a moment of genuine conversion, of spiritual deepening, the entrance to new dimensions of contemplative experience. The monk's experience of existential dread is an experience of the emptiness and lostness of all modern people, but experienced in a particular context and depth. While most people experience this existential dread as boredom or spiritual disorientation, the monk experiences it as a struggle with God in which the power and hope of the Spirit are nevertheless possible. The climate of monastic prayer, Merton writes, is the desert which is removed from the security and routine of ordinary social life and which allows the monk to depend on God alone. The climate is an "inner waste," a heart that has been "humbled and emptied by dread."[18]

Merton goes on to describe the various elements of monastic ascesis and prayer, both liturgical and personal, as patterns and usages designed to deepen both prayer and self-confrontation. He speaks of the rhythm or movement of monastic prayer as an "alternation of darkness and light" and of the need for spiritual direction in order to discern God's grace and to have insight into the obstacles to one's prayer. For such obstacles may have deep roots in one's character. For example, one who has a few natural gifts and a bit of ingenuity can be deluded into thinking that he or she can, by cleverness, learn to master the spiritual life. One can become self-confident and self-complacent, observing oneself, convincing oneself of one's progress. Here, in particular, Zen teaching and the teaching of the desert tradition are alike helpful in their ruthless combat against self-delusion. For in fact, one is imprisoned in oneself.

Or, in another example, one may divide the spiritual or inner life from the rest of one's concrete existence, neglecting or disparaging external concerns or one's relations to others as merely "worldly," sensual, material. Merton comments, "This is bad theology and bad asceticism." For "love of others and openness to others" especially is the "condition for a living and fruitful inner life of thought and love." Or, finally, some may try to make a work of art of their lives simply by following an approved pattern. This encourages them to study themselves in order to shape their lives and remodel themselves, "to tune and re-tune all their inner dispositions" and they end up in "full-time meditation and contemplation of *themselves.*" And so they avoid the risk and dread of the unknown mystery of *God.* Hence the importance of descent into the reality of one's own nothingness in order to shatter self-complacency and allow the reality of God into one's heart.[19]

As Merton develops these now familiar themes, we notice that they are newly set in a more integrated incarnational framework which affirms other people and the created order in itself and as redeemed in Christ. This, however, does not mean that he has abandoned the depth and intensity of the spiritual struggle and the conflict between truth and illusion. Thus he emphasizes, in this final book, the painful purgation which is necessary for growth and relates this to the experience of dread vividly described by the existentialists. In undergoing the humiliation of existential dread, he continues, monks must

> decide whether to go on in the way of prayer under the secret guidance of grace, in the night of pure faith, or whether they will go back to a form of existence in which they can enjoy familiar routines and retain an illusory sense of their own perfect autonomy in perfectly familiar realms.[20]

Citing St. John of the Cross, Merton says that "God brings these people into darkness" so that grace can work in them "passively," purifying that very night itself. Thus the darkening is at the same time an enlightenment. In fact, it is the excessive light of God which is experienced as darkness.

Merton's new incarnationalism also pervades his discussions of liturgical and personal prayer in this last book, despite its focus on purification and dread. He reviews the teachings on prayer of the various classics, always returning to the theme of simple, even constant prayer of the heart, as against the tyrannical imposition of prescribed methods and systems. While a certain measure of asceticism is necessary "to purify and liberate" the

inner self, the goal is to allow God to work in the "rest of contemplation." And this is a contemplation that carries over into
formal, liturgical prayer. Thus liturgical and personal prayer
should be in harmony, not conflict. Even in the Benedictine tradition, where there is some evidence of a conflict between the
two forms of prayer, and between the active and contemplative
lives, it is resolved in a way that reflects the spirit of St. Benedict:
"all life on earth must necessarily combine elements of action and
rest, bodily labor and mental illumination." And so too, although "liturgical prayer is by its nature more 'active,' it may at
any moment be illuminated by contemplative grace."[21]

But it remains apparent that Merton's deepest attraction is to
the spontaneous liberty of purely contemplative prayer. It is in
the "prayer of the heart," he writes, that "we seek first of all the
deepest ground of our identity in God." The intent of such
prayer is not to theorize or reason about God but rather "to gain
an existential grasp, a personal experience of the deepest truths
of life and faith, *finding ourselves in God's truth*." The "dark
night" of suffering and dread purifies these deepest intentions of
the seeker, bringing one to what the monastic fathers called "purity of heart, an unconditional and totally humble surrender to
God, a total acceptance of ourselves. . . . " Purity of heart also
means the surrender of "all deluded images of ourselves, all exaggerated estimates of our own capacities" in the everyday acceptance of God's will in the ordinary demands of life.

> *Purity of heart* is then correlative to a new spiritual identity—the
> "self" as recognized in the context of realities willed by God—purity
> of heart is the enlightened awareness of the new man, as opposed
> to the complex and perhaps rather disreputable fantasies of the "old
> man."[22]

The purpose of prayer as meditation is the uncovering of insight into the self in this new aspect. "Who am I? I am myself
a word spoken by God. Can God speak a word that does not
have any meaning?" Yet one cannot be sure that one's life really
has the meaning intended for it by God. The fact is that God

does not impose this meaning from the outside through custom, routine, society, or law. Rather, Merton asks, in a quite radical change from the rhetoric of total "abandonment" to God's will of his early writing:

> Am I called to *create from within,* with [God], with [God's] grace, a meaning which reflects [God's] truth and makes me [God's] "word" spoken freely in my personal situation? My true identity lies hidden in God's call to my freedom and my response to [God].[23]

The identity of the person is now seen more as a cooperative task in which the creative freedom of the person "conspires" with God's grace to become the self that one is "meant" to be.

While Merton retains, in relation to God's impenetrable mystery, the language of "my own meaninglessness," he writes that one cannot discover the meaning of one's life if one evades the dread which accompanies confrontation with the self and its sham in relation to God. For one's whole life is involved in this turning to God. And one discovers that one's aims usually tend to be artificial and inauthentic insofar as one tries to adjust to certain exterior norms that merely enable one to play an approved role. Even a religious role, like the "imitation of Christ," can become mere impersonation if it is only exterior.

It is dread, "existential dread" in the language and thought world of Sartre, which is the background of this passage. Or it is "monastic dread" in Merton's translation of existentialism into a Christian context. It is a dread which one experiences as one stands alone before God, "without explanation, without theories, completely dependent" on God's grace and mercy. And so prayer should begin with awareness of one's nothingness and helplessness before God. For "finding our heart" and recovering awareness of our inmost identity

> implies recognition that our external, everyday self is to a great extent a mask and a fabrication. It is not our true self. And indeed our true self is not easy to find. It is hidden in obscurity and "nothingness," at the center where we are in direct dependence on God.[24]

The capacity to recognize this "nothingness" of ourselves in relation to God—and thus even the experience of anxiety and dread
—is a grace.

Merton is clear in this book that he has no desire to make a
cult of suffering, self-denial, or sacrifice. But he nevertheless insists that these are necessary for the change of heart or conversion
that is required to make one "new" in Christ. The control of
one's thoughts and desires that is required for interior freedom
does not mean contempt for the world and the ordinary; much
less does it mean resignation to conditions of social injustice. It
does mean freedom and detachment from *inordinate* concerns, a
freedom that frees one really to enjoy the use of good things and
to work against unjust conditions. Christian asceticism is a paradox of suspension between heaven and earth, a necessary suspension that presages something new. For beyond the ascetic life,
the Christian enters into a new realm of the unitive knowledge
of God which corresponds to the suffering of passive purification,
a transcendent kind of knowledge in which the created "self"
which one is seems to disappear in God and to know ordinary
things in God. "In passive purification . . . the self undergoes a
kind of emptying and an apparent destruction, until, reduced to
emptiness, it no longer knows itself apart from God."[25]

Merton describes sacrifice itself as a "way" in which God purifies the self in a fashion that one usually does not understand.
Thus it is better to allow grace to work by accepting the sacrifices
that come naturally in one's life rather than by choosing special
ones. Purification of mind and spirit will gradually enable the
conscious mind "to realize its lack of full autonomy" and in this
process the unconscious will often make its hidden power felt in
strange and disturbing ways. Again, Merton does not hesitate to
name this experience the "dark night" which is necessary not only
in the life of the monk on the way to mature contemplation, but
for anyone who wishes to grow toward spiritual depth. In accepting the sacrifices that life imposes as part of this passive purification, one is drawn out from behind the protective defenses that

one has constructed—even those that might be helpful in ordinary life but which are ultimately limitations to growth.

Through this "testing of the spirit," on the side of contemplative prayer, one comes into the presence of the fully incomprehensible God who can no longer be made into the "object" of one's prayer but is obscurely experienced as subject. This is what is meant by prayer "beyond images." On the side of the self, "it is in proportion as we are known to God that we find our real being and identity in Christ." In this experience, which is one of inner renewal, "an inner transformation brought about by the power of God's merciful love," there occurs the "death" of the self-centered and self-sufficient ego and the appearance of a new and liberated self who lives and acts in the Spirit. And Merton warns that one can even go through a false imitation of this experience in which the old self, "the calculating and autonomous ego," simply confirms itself once again. Thus any falsity or lying to oneself is especially harmful at this point, in fact spiritually disastrous in its infidelity to the self as well as to God.[26]

In the final chapters of *Contemplative Prayer,* Merton relates the theme of dread to his theology of original sin. In the last analysis, he says, it is not only the created "nothingness" or the contingency of human life, in relation to the incomprehensible God known through the grace of revelation, that is the reason for existential or monastic dread. It is the fact that relationship to God as the source of one's being has been "freely repudiated." One discerns in oneself the reality of sin as *original sin,* not just as particular sins, in the experience of dread. It is the pervasive depth of sin in one's very self that presses one to acknowledge that one has already rebelled against God and that explains the self-deception and subtle religious egoism that can be found even in religious people.

> Sometimes one feels that a well-intentioned and inculpable atheist is in many ways better off—and gives more glory to God—than some people whose bigoted complacency and inhumanity to others are signs of the most obvious selfishness![27]

Hence the need, in the experience of existential dread, not only "to recover an awareness of our creaturehood; we must also repair the injury done to truth and to love by this repudiation, this infidelity." But of course, one cannot do this on one's own; there is "no way." Here Merton applies the "cosmic" theology of original sin of the Eastern fathers, which he had used in his early writings to describe humankind's common "fall" from contemplative union with God as the loss of "likeness" to God, in a different way to the individual in the experience of existential dread. Beyond the dread of facing one's own contingency or death or non-being, there is the final dreadful awareness of alienation from God and from oneself, awareness of a deep rebellion against or failure to respond to the truth that stems from a kind of *malice* in oneself.

> The real import of dread is to be sought in an infidelity to a personal demand of which one is at least dimly aware: the failure to meet a challenge, to fulfill a certain possibility which demands to be met and fulfilled. The price of this failure to measure up to an existential demand of one's own life is a general sense of failure, of guilt.[28]

When Merton introduces the notion of guilt here, he is speaking at a theological level, beyond "mere neurotic anxiety," and beyond psychology. But his is a theology that has experiential implications: one has a sense of failure, a personal awareness of one's own infidelity in not facing truth, and in not "giving back . . . a fair return for all that has been given. . . . " And there is nothing one can do to repair the failure; one is helpless and the dread is intensified by one's utter dependence. This is the extreme of dread: it is "nothingness" and "night" in the awareness of "infidelity to the truth of our life," an unrepentable sense of "antagonism between the self and God" because of an estrangement in our own distorted attachment to a " 'self' which is mysterious and illusory." Even the sincere reception of the sacraments of the church in faith, while enabling belief that one is restored to God, cannot liberate one from the dreadful experience so long as one clings "to the empty illusion of a separate self" which is always "inclined to resist God." Theologically, the *effects* of original sin remain in the Christian after baptism and Merton describes the *experience* of those effects in the spiritual life as "an inclination to sin and rebellion, an inclination to falsity and to evasion."[29]

This experience of dread at this radical depth is different, Merton notes, from remorse. For remorse is for something specific that one has done or failed to do. But dread is the "worst emptiness of the faithful Christian" who has really tried conscientiously to do what is required in the tasks of life and still realizes even more deeply a radical wrongness: "the naked dread that is indefinite because it seems to be coextensive with [one's] whole being and [one's] whole life." This dread is constituted further by a sense that even God is no longer a refuge. God is experienced as hostile, an enemy, or finally as emptiness. And thus one further begins to dread the loss of faith. One struggles to regain a sense of self in the familiar routines until even the power to struggle is lost.[30]

Merton's counsel, at this brink of doubt and despair, "over the face of a thinly veiled abyss of disoriented nothingness," is to accept this state as the genuine climate of serious prayer, to drop all arrogance, and to submit to the incomprehensibility of the situation and even become content with it. "This deep dread and night must then be seen for what it is: not as punishment, but as purification and as grace." It is grace because the experience of dread enables realization that, no matter what progress one thinks one has made, whatever one is or has is nothing and can fail. One can never be "sure" on the basis of the past and one's achievements. In language reminiscent of Heidegger's existentialism, Merton suggests that one must turn from the past toward the future.

> We are open to God and to [God's] mercy in the inscrutable future and our trust is entirely in [God's] grace, which will support our liberty in the emptiness where we will confront unforeseen deci-

sions. Only when we have descended in dread to the center of our own nothingness, by [God's] grace . . . and guidance, can we be led by [God] . . . to find [God] in losing ourselves.[31]

Thus Merton returns to the familiar theme of loss of self, so central in his interpretation of both Christian mysticism and Zen Buddhism. Here he describes self-loss in stark, experiential terms: it is dereliction, a kind of hell. But it is also, in the words of the twelfth-century Cistercian, Isaac of Stella, a "hell of mercy," not of wrath. For in this hell as one experiences one's final nothingness, one can finally relax the "determined grasp of our empty self" and "escape from the cage of emptiness, despair, dread, and sin into the infinite space and freedom of grace and mercy." But, Merton warns, if there is any "vestige of self" remaining which can realize that it "has arrived," then one can be certain that the experience of dread will return "until all self-sufficiency and self-complacency are destroyed." The freedom from self-consciousness that Merton envisions, that he finds in the Christian spiritual tradition and that is confirmed by Zen teaching and experience is so revolutionary that he uses the biblical imagery of the Day of the Lord to suggest its radical character:

> For the Lord of hosts has a day against all that is proud and lofty, against all that is lifted up and high. And the haughtiness of man shall be humbled, and the pride of men shall be brought low; and the Lord alone will be exalted in that day. And the idols shall utterly pass away. (Is. 2:11, 17, 18)[32]

The lesson of this dread for the life of prayer, as Merton concludes in *Contemplative Prayer,* is that all forms of meditation or contemplation which enable one to evade the bitter truth of the self, to preserve one's familiar roles, will need to be "unlearned in dread." Any pattern that closes a person to those others who refuse to collaborate in one's self-idolatry and illusions, any routine that allows one simply to be satisfied with the past means a prayer that is a "factory for alibis." One recognizes genuine prayer when it is an experience of struggle with the sense of inauthenticity and falsity in the self. In his existentialist mood, Merton says that this prayer will be marked by willingness to forget the past and by openness to the needs of the present, in the risk of new ideas and new solutions.[33]

Having explored the depths of existential or monastic dread, Merton responds to the charge he imagines he hears from his critics that this emphasis on dread is simply negative, a neurotic symptom of the excessive self-concern of contemporary people. Moreover, his religious critics will say that it would be better to counsel monks and other Christians to turn to the liturgy, the objective worship of the church, in order to be lifted out of such narcissistic preoccupation. But Merton counters that the inner emptiness he explores also enters into the experience of liturgy and can be the experience of whole monastic communities, congregations, and parishes and not just that of the solitary seeker. "Unless the Christian participates to some degree in the dread, the sense of loss, the anguish, the dereliction and the destitution of the Crucified, he [or she] cannot really enter into the mystery of the liturgy."[34]

Further, Merton relates the theme of dread in prayer to the Marxist criticism that this dread is simply the expression of the guilt and false consciousness or the "inner dishonesty of an alienated class." He admits that the spirit of individualism that is connected with the economy and culture of the West has had negative effects on much Christian prayer. Individualistic prayer, however, is precisely the kind that "closes in on itself without dread" and rests in its own satisfactions. It is content with devotionalism and sentimentality and resists the "summons to communal witness and collective human response to God" that the liturgy represents. It is intimate, private, and quite opposite to that "true personalism" which entails free self-disposal toward the other in openness (Gabriel Marcel's *disponibilité*). In fact, it is dread that can deliver the Christian from individualism in prayer as in life, "for the dread and guilt of the sinner show [one] more clearly than anything else [the] need for reconciliation with God in and through reconciliation with [other people]." Dread and the dark night, in personal and communal prayer, liberate the self and the community from the smug self-complacency of the privileged which places ultimate faith in its own nation, race or class, and renders God as the status quo.[35]

In this powerful little book, Merton's thought reaches to the whole of Christian existence. *Contemplative Prayer* insists that the experience of dread or the dark night is integral to the life of contemplation and the emergence of the true self of the monk as of the ordinary Christian. And contemplation is integral to liturgical prayer and the emergence of the community of authentic persons who, in their self-forgetfulness and even self-loss, are enabled to pray as the communal body of Christ and to bear effective collective witness against the sinfulness—the social injustice and patterns of privilege and domination—of the world.[36]

6

_____

THE STORY OF THE SELF

The question of the real, or true, or authentic self engaged Merton throughout his life as a monk and writer. He found in the notion of the hidden self known only to God an important focal point and symbol that could integrate the active elements of the search for the realized experience of union with God in prayer with its purely gratuitous character as a gift of God.

Merton's successive reformulations of the issue make evident his dissatisfaction with merely technical or abstract theological categories to describe the complexities of the false and true selves; he is always seeking more immediate, compelling, experiential, and symbolic terms in which to explore his theme. True, Merton consistently seeks out the theological underpinnings for his own experience in prayer and for his various formulations of the problem of the self in the writings of the church and monastic fathers and in the descriptive statements on contemplative prayer recorded by the Christian mystics. But he typically transposes theological categories to the plane of spiritual experience, as when he connects the doctrine of original sin with the patristic idea of a fall from an original contemplative union with God, or translates the mystical "dark night" into the contemporary experience of "existential anxiety," which he then calls "existential dread" or "monastic dread."

Indeed, Merton's interest in the question of the self is radically experiential. In his autobiographical reflections he sees his own religious pilgrimage as a quest for the selflessness of "non-identity," an attempt to "lose himself" both as a monk and as a writer. The texts we have examined show Merton's intensifying interest in the experiential implications of such religious selflessness. In his own religious search, we might speculate, he finds the "self" to be a source of constant anxiety, always "in the way" as he tries to approach "what the books say" about the depths of prayer. And yet he recognizes the self also as a central gift of God's creation, sanctified and destined for transformation in Christ. The realization of such transformation or "rebirth" is paradoxically both the task of the Christian, especially the monk, and a gift for which one can only prepare oneself in waiting, responsiveness, and receptivity.

The analogies Merton finds between Christian mysticism, modern psychology, existentialism, and Zen teaching and practice sharpen dramatically his own formulations about the external and inner selves, false autonomy and the receptive grace of the cosmic wisdom intuition. These analogies are rooted in experience, not theory, although Merton is never scornful of theory and always includes careful theoretical discussion in his own study and analysis of the various religious traditions. But his persistent focus on experience goes far to explain his enduring popularity among ordinary readers of all kinds, whether Christian or not, and his classic status among the religious writers of our times.

Merton's concern for the integrity of experience and his canny writer's feeling for a language that can communicate to contemporary people the riches of the ancient spiritual traditions leads him to fuse theological and psychological perspectives in his writing. With particular power he elaborates the goal of contemplation as a final, paradoxical, renunciation of both experience and fulfillment in a union with God that is focused so wholly outside the self that only the language of self-loss or identification with God can describe it.[1]

Throughout his various texts on the theme of the self, Merton's thought remains rooted in the personalist theory of Jacques Maritain with its bipolar understanding of the human being: the

material pole is expressed in the term *individual* and the spiritual
pole in the term *person*. When the material side dominates the
whole, there is an *individualism* that Merton describes as a sham,
illusion, and fully "disreputable" because it is, in his understanding, the inferior side of the self. It is the mere ego-self mas-
querading as the whole. This domination of the whole by the
self-centered ego-self he calls the "false self" or the merely external self, because it is indeed a "lie" that denies the truth of the
real person as spirit. In a genuine *personalism,* the spirit is the
heart and controlling center of the integral human being.

Thus Merton can write of the struggle in contemporary society
—whether in the monastery or in the world outside its walls—to
find the true or inner self. The struggle is a profound one because,
in fact, the inner self of spirit is, in Maritain's terms, the true,
metaphysical self. It is immaterial, imperceptible to "society,"
the ground of personal wholeness hidden beneath the external
roles or masks the self wears. It is the image of this stark polarity,
perhaps, that led Merton himself to search, in the solitude and
silence of the monastery, for the true, inner self in the life of
contemplation. For the contemplative tradition maintains that
it is only in finding God that one finds oneself. Thus *Seeds of
Contemplation,* for example, seems to suggest contemplative
prayer as the "answer" to the search for the self, as the "key" to
experiential knowledge of God and to self-discovery.

Merton's own experience of contemplative prayer in the
monastery, however, teaches him that even such a radical commitment to contemplative life does not automatically bring res-
olution to the question of the self. Once in the monastery, he
discovers that he has brought *himself* with him from the noisy
and distracting world. The monastery remains in the world and
the world is in the monastery. And the problem of the self remains in either context. In 1966 Merton wrote in a popular
Catholic magazine for lay readers:

> I am . . . a man in the modern world. In fact, I *am* the world just
> as you are! Where am I going to look for the world first of all if

not in myself? . . . As long as I imagine that the world is something to be "escaped" in the monastery—that wearing a special costume and following a quaint observance takes me "out of the world," I am dedicating my life to an illusion.[2]

Through the texts we have examined it seems apparent that Merton's monastic experience taught him that the distinction between the individual and the person is far more complex than he had initially suggested in his early writing. He discovers, for one thing, that the false self, though still a broadly satisfying and accurate designation for one's material or individualist side as it seeks a false autonomy or domination of the whole, is not simply opposed to spirit, as one's conscious, religious self. Rather, in subtle and self-deceiving ways, the false self can dominate the spirit even under the guise of "good" motives and "religious" or "spiritual" intentions. With its ego-centered focus the false self constantly plans and projects, in ever more clever and disguised fashion and in ways that thwart authentic love of God and neighbor and truly selfless prayer. Awareness of the continual machinations of the false self leads Merton to use the psychological categories of the narcissistic and neurotic self, finding in this rhetoric a language for some of the extreme manifestations of false religiosity: fanaticism, obsession, compulsion, all of which indicate a lack of genuine psychological freedom.

At this level of psychology, there is a further complication as Merton discovers that autonomy is not always the false religious autonomy castigated by the classical monastic and mystical tradition. In fact, one simple definition of *neurosis* is a lack of psychological autonomy or ego strength. In his later work with novices and young monks, Merton learns that autonomy at the psychological level is a necessary precondition for an authentic spiritual or contemplative life. One cannot offer to God a self that one does not already, in some measure, possess. Thus, while the neurotic self represents for Merton a psychological extreme, a manifestation of the false or empirical or external self, it also means that self as distorted, as lacking a necessary and good autonomy. In his work with the young Americans who came to the monastery, perhaps Merton discovered that he himself in fact possessed a good measure of this substratum of personal autonomy that is absolutely necessary for even entering into the spiritual battle of the self that the monastic and mystical tradition describes.

In fact, it may be precisely because of his own strong psychological autonomy, the highly developed ego strength of Merton the creative thinker and writer, that the spiritual traditions of both Christianity and Zen are so attractive to him. Possessed of a very strong sense of self, he struggled to lose himself, in his writing and in his prayer.[3] At the fully spiritual level, the battle with the self, even to the point of existential or monastic dread, must be played out before it can produce realization of the kind of self-loss that is the fullness of contemplative prayer.

One must be careful to distinguish these different levels in Merton's discussions. When he refers to the neurotic or narcissistic self, he is referring to the extreme psychological manifestations of the false self. When he refers simply to the empirical, external, or weak self, he is using Maritain's metaphysical language to point to the merely individual, "material" self. When he refers to the true or false self of the spiritual tradition, he is using theological language. And at this level of the whole, the false self can sometimes include both the metaphysical foundation of the weak, but imperious, external self and the psychological manifestations of the narcissistic or neurotic self. It is important to differentiate the context or level in which Merton uses these terms and to remember that he always uses them in suggestive, nontechnical, symbolic ways. They are not simply synonyms for the true and false selves of the spiritual plane. Yet these levels are united, in their differentiated meaning, in the one self that struggles to find God in the Christian life of prayer and so to come to the self-loss, at the theological level of the Christian mystical tradition, or the breakthrough, at the metaphysical level, in Merton's interpretation of Zen *satori* or Buddhist *nirvana*.

While Merton is not suggesting that everyone must be a contemplative monk or practice Zen, he does believe that the problem of the real and illusory selves is universal and that elements of the kind of consciousness described in the Christian contemplative tradition and in Zen teaching offer important insight to an age in search of the self. In contrast to the self-centered and acquisitive "appetites" or patterns of modern Western consciousness, in which the empirical ego is dominant, he sketches the unitive and selfless experience of the Christian mystical and Zen traditions. And he suggests that an outgrowth of the unitive experience of contemplative prayer is an integrated, holistic, everyday consciousness that has, through spiritual discipline, recovered its created innocence. For he sees in the ancient Christian, the medieval mystical, and Eastern traditions an analogous vision of inner, natural, cosmic wholeness that offers an important answer to the deepest problems of Western consciousness.

To be sure, Merton often paints the contrast between East and West, ancient and modern, natural and artificial, "true" and "false" in stark, perhaps oversimple terms in his various writings. But he works not so much through systematic or logical argument as by image and symbol to suggest the manifold dimensions these contrasts might entail in different contexts. With regard to the self, his later convictions about the inner, cosmic wholeness of creation mean that truth and integrity are found not simply in "adjusting to" external reality but rather in responding to one's deepest and most natural intuitions of being in oneself, in others, in God. Ultimately it is the ordinary and familiar self of Merton's later reflections who recovers, through the struggle of becoming and the dark night of existential dread, the original affirmation given in one's limited, relational, created · being and is thus open to the transformation offered, in Christian terms, in the economy of grace, sacrament, and prayer. Such prayer is both communal and contemplative, personal and liturgical—a responsive prayer that is a harmonious alternation of activity and receptivity.

This, we might speculate, is fully authentic religious self-affirmation and autonomy in Merton's scheme of thought and experience. Consent to this original and intrinsic givenness of one's created being differs sharply, in Merton's work, from the unfreedom of "servility" (a false and external dependence on persons, events, appearances, roles). It is rather the radical inner acceptance of oneself as created being—that is, oneself as gifted with a liberty that implies both autonomy and essential receptivity to God and to others.

Merton's autobiographical reflections demonstrate clearly this paradox of "infinite" spiritual liberty and acceptance of one's created, relational, and earthly limits. This liberty and acceptance imply freedom from absolutizing in regard to religious ideology, spiritual technique, or projected ideals of the self, plus an ability to accept one's dark self or shadow in the finding of the inner self in God. This is Merton's "cosmic humility." His quest for the truth of the self—inner, contemplative, hidden—finally means recovery of the unselfconscious, wise, childlike identity that was given in creation. In symbolic terms, this is for him "wisdom," "return from exile," "the recovery of paradise," or being found, once again, by God. It seems to be a goal never entirely reached by Merton but an ideal continually sought. For autobiographically, on his Asian journey, Merton writes of his visit with Chatral Rimpoche in India:

> He said he had meditated in solitude for thirty years or more and had not attained to perfect emptiness and I said I hadn't either. The unspoken or half-spoken message of the talk was our complete understanding of each other as people who were somehow *on the edge* of great realization and knew it and were trying, somehow or other, to go out and get lost in it—and that it was a grace for us to meet one another.[4]

Or perhaps the great realization did come about, in some sense, for Merton, just shortly before his death. For later in his journey he describes his visit to Polonnaruwa, in Ceylon (Sri Lanka), to see the huge statues of the Buddha.

Looking at those figures I was suddenly, almost forcibly, jerked clean out of the habitual, half-tried vision of things, and an inner cleanness, clarity, as if exploding from the rocks themselves, became evident and obvious. . . . Surely with Mahabalipuram and Polonnaruwa my Asian pilgrimage has come clear and purified itself. I mean, I know and have seen what I was obscurely looking for. I don't know what else remains but I have seen and pierced through the shadow and the disguise.[5]

Perhaps, then, the long-sought realization in personal experience did occur before the end of Merton's own final pilgrimage.

Merton's many formulations of the problem of the self and his autobiographical reflections on his own identity and spiritual quest invite analysis from several perspectives. In psychological terms, there are analogies with Freudian theory: the empirical or psychological ego and its struggle for autonomy from the pull of unconscious wishes and motivations rooted in the past of childhood. In this framework, there is the possibility of the emergence of the strong, autonomous ego over against the subtleties and distortions of self-deception, the possibility of a psychic health manifested in the ability to work and to love, productively and creatively. Merton's writing and the open, world-embracing character of his later years surely give evidence of an unusually creative and full capacity for love and work.[6]

Perhaps even stronger is the correspondence with Jungian theory suggested by the pattern of individuation from the ego to the self, through conscious acceptance of the dark self or shadow (for a man, the *anima*, his feminine side) and the importance of the *persona* and religious myth in this process. One could argue that Merton's highly individuated self, both as an untypical monk and as a creative writer, exemplify Jung's psychological pattern very aptly. Or Erikson's developmental stages are suggestive to the interpreter: from the initial need for basic trust in infancy to the identity crisis of youth (important stages in Merton's life because of the death of his mother while he was still a child and the death of his father when he was an adolescent in England), through the problems of intimacy and generativity in adulthood. Clearly there is a progression in his life from the "other-directed" discipline of the monastic community (obedience to the abbot and the rules of a highly regulated schedule of prayer and work) to the "inner-directed" strength and liberty of the hermit, "on his own feet" yet guided by the Holy Spirit within.[7]

Theologically, Merton's analyses of the self portray the Christian scheme of creation, sin, incarnation and grace, and the death and resurrection of Christ in terms of individual experience, especially in prayer. The estrangement of sin is experienced in the fragmentation of the self because of its fall from the truth of contemplative union with God for which it is created. It is also experienced in the existential or monastic dread which will finally characterize the struggle of prayer. Conversion to God as the ultimate focus outside the self, entailing both love of God and love of other persons, is in fact recovery of the self in conscious awareness of the presence of God within the self: one becomes a *person* united with others in Christ, in a liberation from individualism that implies a new creation or new being, yet a self that is, nevertheless, the person one was always meant to be.

In the terms of traditional Catholic mystical theology, there are indications in Merton's writings of the three stages of the purgative, illuminative, and unitive "ways," of the movement from vocal to interior prayer, and the movement from active to passive contemplation. But there is no indication of a simple line of "progress" in Merton's thought, nor of the dominance of any particular religious model or preconceived pattern of development. In an important sense one is always a beginner: in Merton's last writing, he is still exploring the depths of purgation, the purification of the "dark night" of the senses and the spirit in the experience of dread. Certainly Merton's life and writing testify to the importance of a religious framework of meaning that disposes the individual, through its patterns of worship, discipline, self-criticism, and self-knowledge, for the new liberty of authentic love of God and other persons. These psychological and religious "explanations" surely aid in understanding Merton's life and thought.

But Merton's experience and reflection on the problem of the self are also resistant to any tight systematic theory, and they witness to both the value and the ambiguous incompleteness of any psychological pattern, theological framework, or model of interiority in charting the becoming of the person. While Merton's early writings on the self may be said to reflect the ancient Augustinian model of sin and grace in human experience, his successive explorations of the problem of the self and his repeated struggles with the question of identity mark his thought as peculiarly modern or contemporary in their never quite resolved character. It is not Merton's appropriation of Zen or of existentialism that makes him a classic and symbolic figure for our time, but the way in which any traditional religious (or contemporary psychological) answer constantly is met with new questions and is creatively transformed in each new situation.

Merton's particular genius lies in his fusion of religious or metaphorical discourse and psychological, experiential language in a holistic symbolic vision that reveals how any pattern or system falls short of the mysterious uniqueness of the person. For his successive theories of the self describe the struggle of moving from ego or self to authentic personhood, not simply as fidelity to an abstract model or religious self-conception but as an ever-changing quest for fidelity to concrete, individual, historical life, both personal and communal. Merton's theoretical and personal expression of the tangible particularity of the contemporary experience of selfhood is peculiarly modern, so like our own, in its historical, developmental, and protean character.

Moving through Merton's discussions of the self one senses an important shift from the idea of the *discovery* of the hidden self, preconceived by God, to that of the self's continual and responsive *creation* or re-creation of itself in changing personal and historical contexts. In Merton's later thought *creativity* is newly conceived. We find that the renunciation of our false self, the emptying of self in the likeness to Christ . . . brings us to the threshold of that true creativity in which God . . . the creator, works in us and through us.[8]

The map that emerges in Merton's thought is one of changing theological contexts as well, as he moves from the nature/super-nature dichotomy of his early writing to the patristic notion of the lost likeness to God, and then to the wisdom intuition of creation. The wisdom intuition, however, is not attained without going through the crucible of the dark night or the experience of existential or monastic dread, a spiritual battle which demands a healthy psychological autonomy as its own precondition and the precondition as well for the final gift of self to God and to others.

The question of the self is never quite resolved for Merton because it could not be, so long as he continued to live, to experience, and to give written expression to that experience. The radically temporal quality of his work is such that no identity, and no text, could wholly embody in any simple way the significance of his life or suggest any "finished" character in his thought on the subject of the self. It is this taste and texture of the unique, unrepeatable, and always changing historical experience of the self in Merton's writing that touches a contemporary nerve and makes him a classic figure in recent religious history. He captures, in first-order, religious language, the central symbol of the self in the changing shape of the religious search in our times. In its particularity, the untypical life of a monk and writer of the twentieth century strikes a note of universality.[9]

In Merton's spiritual and symbolic universe there is both continuity and change. The continuity is accounted for by his personal immersion in the writings of the church and monastic fathers and the mystical tradition of his own Christian formation and his successive reinterpretations of the great themes of these classics in the light of his own changing experience. In Merton's early writing—*Seeds of Contemplation,* for example—his own dramatic conversion to Christianity is the lens through which he views Christian life and his newly adopted monastic goal: the realized experience of finding God and so of finding the true self. The symbols of the true and false selves are appropriate for expressing his experience at this time, in perfect correspondence with the stark contrasts he draws between the world and the monastery, the corrupt city and the holy community in the country, and between nature and grace (or the natural and the supernatural). It is hardly straining this early perspective to see the contrast finally as one of good and evil, when one recalls Merton's disparagement of the self that was born of his mother and of the people who still "crawl about in time," over against the integrity of the saint and the dedication of the monk whose whole life is given over to seeking God.

The nature/supernature distinction provides an apt framework for opposing good and evil in Merton's early work as a spiritual writer, and for expressing his profound joy in the discovery of the adventure of the spiritual life and in his own monastic and solitary vocation. It is a joy he communicates vividly and enthusiastically in his writing. But the nature/supernature distinction seems too simple a contrast to satisfy him for very long, especially in relation to the classical Christian doctrines of creation, Incarnation, and the Mystical Body which Merton absorbed in his study of theology and which he then began to incorporate in his writing. For these doctrines imply the goodness of creation, a goodness redeemed and transformed by Christ, and the intrinsic unity of all people in Christ, all of whom are loved by God and worthy of genuine human love. But the doctrines remain somewhat abstract for Merton in his early writing as he insists on the necessity of withdrawal, of forgetting others in the life of prayer.

Thus Merton turns, in *The Silent Life,* to another Christian framework of interpretation, the doctrine of the human person as created in the image and likeness of God. The patristic reading of this biblical symbol, that the image of God remains in the person while the likeness of contemplative union with God (the reality of paradise) is lost in the exile of original sin, offers Merton a new way of conceiving the purpose of the monastic life, which is for him at this time the most perfect form of Christian life. Finding God and finding the true self are taken with utter seriousness, he says, only by the monk. The monk learns through the discipline of monastic vows, especially obedience and the *conversio morum,* but also by the practice of poverty, humility, and detachment, that a "loss of self" is entailed in wholehearted response to God.

At this stage in his life Merton still conceives of the ordinary self as false in contrast to the true self of monastic holiness and "purity of heart." The false self is seen as the "individual" of Maritain's scheme of thought, the side of the self that is rooted in matter. And in Merton's expression at this time, it can appear as almost totally opposed to the spiritual side that is the "person" meant to be realized in Christ. But perhaps even then he saw that this contrast of "individual" and "person" is too radical an interpretation of Maritain's Thomism, too simple a distinction for the complexity of human becoming.

In "The Inner Experience" the polar contrast of true and false selves gives way to a new expression. Merton begins to write more of the inner and exterior selves, finding in this language a more satisfying experiential terminology that allows him to explore the psychological ramifications of "identity," and in a more complex theological way as well. Within these categories, the true self is the inner self, a hidden self, the metaphysical self or spirit of Maritain's personalism. Merton complicates his own pattern by reference to the psychological theory of the unconscious and suggests the spiritual importance of consciously accepting and integrating one's dark self or negative side as a way toward full self-acceptance.

And in "The Inner Experience" Merton makes his initial textual reference to Zen teaching about self-loss. Still wary of collapsing distinctions between Christianity and other religions,

Merton uses Maritain's understanding of the metaphysical self to elaborate his own interpretation of the inner self and its uncovery through Zen meditation or Christian contemplation. Christian contemplation goes further than Zen experience, he maintains, beyond the discovery of the inner or metaphysical self, to an awareness of the presence of God in the inner self.

Conjectures of a Guilty Bystander represents the real textual turning point in the written record of Merton's own spiritual experience, as well as in his more theoretical reflections on the problematic of the self. His celebrated "Louisville vision," with its important connections to the prose poem *Hagia Sophia* in which Merton grapples with the powerful theme of the feminine (an early symbol for him of temptation and sin), is central in this turn in Merton's experience. One senses a new openness in his writing. In *Conjectures* Merton makes his new and surprising observation that some natural appetites are good and that it is usually better to do the ordinary human thing than to try to perform like an angel. As he awakens from his own dream of "spurious isolation," he joyfully recognizes that he is a "member of the human race" and that he loves other people. The experience makes him want to laugh aloud, so great is his sense of release from his former self, the self of pious withdrawal as both monk and writer.

Merton's reading of Pasternak's *Dr. Zhivago* and his critical interpretation of its creational and cosmic themes, especially in the female figure of Lara, is surely important in his new affirmation of the wisdom of creation and of nature itself. And Merton now describes the goal of contemplation in new language as the intuition of wisdom. He also registers his own critical wisdom about posing any ideology, including religious ideology, as a preconceived pattern, system, or theory to which the self is expected to conform. He now describes even the monastic discipline, with its rules and usages, as helpful and perhaps necessary for beginners, but as a "school of liberty," the monastery is also meant to release its students to the spontaneity of interior growth and the independence of maturity.

Conjectures of a Guilty Bystander also reflects Merton's new attention to the acute problems of the American world outside the monastery: its violence and racism, the feigned innocence of its sometimes oppressive history, its pressures toward conformism. Merton's reflections on the crucial social issues of the 1960s mean that the problem of the self is newly cast as the problem of a false autonomy taught by American culture, particularly through the mass media. People are led to believe they can have anything they want and so become knotted up in their own desires and their own selves. And when they discover that they cannot have all that they want, they are led to despair, become suicidal in their very affluence. And yet the things the human person really needs—love, meaning, self-respect—cannot simply be had for the taking. Rather, they are gifts, and one needs to prepare oneself, in receptivity and responsiveness, for receiving them. It is in this context, Merton believes, that the wisdom traditions of the world religions may have something of the "night spirit" and the "dawn breath" that the world desperately needs for the development of more human patterns of life.

This receptivity or responsiveness, however, is not passivity, especially in the face of massive social injustice. On the contrary, one is called to create in oneself, through the workings of God's grace, a creative dissent that is critical of the injustices and distortions of one's society and culture. This creative dissent entails the ability to see beyond the artificial patterns of identity that mass society imposes and, when necessary, to express personal autonomy in a refusal to conform. And, among all the religious traditions, none may be better able to offer aid in transcending culturally imposed roles and artificial identity than Zen teaching and practice.[10]

Zen and the Birds of Appetite and the short but powerful essay "Day of a Stranger" record the new and more joyful Merton as well as his clear dissent from a society of violence and consumerism. There is a new freedom and humor in his writing, perhaps inspired by the wonderful humor, impudence, and comic iconoclasm of Zen. It is as though Merton has come to the realization of an element, at least, of the self-forgetfulness that he has long sought and that allows the real liberty of the created self to emerge. In Merton's interpretation both Christianity and Zen ruthlessly deny that the ego-self in its subjectivity is or can be the center of some extraordinary experience, while both advocate the real possibility of discovering the true self in meditation and contemplation.

At each point of Merton's explorations into the experiential dimensions of Zen he continually returns to the classic mystical sources of Christianity and questions about whether Eastern or Western traditions of self-loss can offer any real wisdom to a world shaped by the Cartesian ego and its extremes of self-consciousness and self-assertion. Despite contemporary Christianity's emphasis on a more dynamic, existential, and biblical framework of encounter and event, he believes that the ancient Christian traditions of contemplation and the medieval understanding of mystical intuition, like Zen teaching and practice, may yet provide possibilities for a different kind of *consciousness* in our overmechanized and competitive world. The possibilities are not great, he believes, but perhaps the new interest in interreligious dialogue offers some hope for the recovery of the "intuition of being" that is, in Merton's understanding, the common base of the ancient mystical traditions of wisdom, both Eastern and Western. He further suggests:

> Though Catholic monasticism is less frankly contemplative, it is in a better position for dialogue with Asia at the moment because of the climate of openness following Vatican II. Christian monasticism has a tradition of adaptation and comprehension with regard to Greek philosophy, and many Catholics realize that this could also apply very well to Hindu and Buddhist philosophies, disciplines, experiences. An articulate minority exists. It is ready for free and productive communication.[11]

Contemplation in a World of Action and *Contemplative Prayer* register the practical and the mystical sides of Merton's thought once again in his own Christian tradition. In the first of these texts, his concern to deepen the interior focus of contemporary monasticism in the context of renewal leads him to reflect on psychological autonomy as a precondition necessary for mature contemplative experience, that is, the spiritual finding of God and of the real self. Merton astutely analyzes the problems of the young Americans who come to the monastery ostensibly to seek God but who are really searching for themselves in an adolescent identity crisis. Such young people, he reasons, must be prepared for monastic culture by a new kind of education to help them establish their own psychological identities before embarking on the spiritual quest of God.

Only when this fundamental psychological autonomy is established can the rhetoric of the contemplative tradition about loss of self in God make sense and the goal of "final" or "transcultural" integration become a real possibility. Only a strong self can sustain the dialectical insight that enables one to be at home in today's pluralistic global religious world and to find continued nourishment in one's own tradition while being open to the wisdom and experience of all the world's religions. That such a dialectical insight and cosmic wisdom is possible is demonstrated in Merton's own life and by his writing, especially in its focus on experience itself rather than dogma or abstract theory.

Moreover, in *Contemplation in a World of Action,* a radical change in Merton's vision of the contemplative life can be noted, as well as the continuity of his interpretation of that life not as a static form or external structure but as a dynamic process of growth and self-discovery. The title of another essay in the book raises a question of the post-Vatican II church: "Is the Contemplative Life Finished?" In other words, does the new Christian perspective on active involvement in history and the *praxis* of faith in the world mean the end of the contemplative tradition as it developed in the classic figures and texts of ancient and medieval times? Merton writes that if the contemplative life is conceived as a "life of withdrawal, tranquility, retirement, silence," it may well be finished. But if it is really understood in its dynamic meaning as the task and the gift of self-discovery, then its traditional monastic form may well disappear, but not its inner reality.

> Do we keep ourselves from action and change in order to learn techniques for entering into a kind of static present reality which is there and which we have to learn to penetrate? Is contemplation an objective static "thing," like a building, for which there is a key? Do you hunt for this key, find it, then unlock the door and enter? . . . [But] the contemplative life isn't something objective that is "there" and to which, after fumbling around, you finally gain access. [It] is a dimension of our subjective existence. Discovery of the contemplative life is a new self-discovery. One might say that it is the flowering of a deeper identity on an entirely different plane from a mere psychological discovery, a paradoxical new identity that is found only in loss of self. To find one's self by losing one's self; that is part of contemplation.[12]

Merton's shift from his own earlier vision of contemplation as a form of structured withdrawal, as a "key" or "answer" to the problems of contemporary life, to a deeper focus on his other early theme of interior self-discovery, suggests that the heart of the contemplative life is not finished, but will find new forms and patterns in the radically incarnational and world-affirming vision of post-Vatican II Christianity. The heart of the contemplative life will emerge wherever persons probe deeply the question of the self and the question of God in openness to concrete history as the world of the self's experience.

In *Contemplative Prayer,* Merton indeed finds new nourishment in his own tradition of the fathers and the mystics as he interprets the "existential anxiety" of modernity as "existential dread" or "monastic dread." The experience of dread, so vividly evoked by the existentialist philosophers, especially Kierkegaard, Heidegger, Sartre, and Camus, is a new frame through which Merton interprets the "dark night" of the mystical tradition. It is a brilliant rereading and contemporary interpretation of that tradition's description of the awesome struggle that takes place in the depths of prayer as one comes to know God and the self. In this book, Merton takes his own place within the Christian mystical tradition of classic writers as he describes the experience of sin as refusal of the challenge that authentic Christianity and monasticism present, a refusal of the struggle with the self that realization of the presence of God enjoins.

Despite the forbidding character of the dread which Merton describes as the climate of monastic prayer, there is a definite undertone of joy and liberation in his last reflections on the life of prayer and self-discovery. This undertone becomes overt and dominant in Merton's more immediate personal reflections in *The Asian Journal,* in which his own most intense experiences of self-realization, at least as his literary reflections record them, are given expression. These experiences take place in the lands that are the birthplace of the earliest recorded traditions of self-discovery and interior liberation. And they suggest that Merton found some answer to the great question that he hoped his journey would provide.

In whatever context of interpretation and experience that Merton wrote, he found the becoming of the true self, both as a constant personal question and as a universal symbol for the depth of religious experience, a singularly evocative way of pointing toward the complexity of a mature spirituality in contemporary life. In each case this becoming is as unique as it was in his own untypical experience. In every person it is a unique historical struggle to find, within and yet beyond interior discipline, self-conception, or religious system, the particular integrity that is the self or person symbolized by the enigmatic phrases: "what one is meant to be," and "I live, now not I, but Christ lives in me," and "your original face before you were born."

In these explorations Merton appropriates the Christian symbols of death and resurrection—as self-loss and recovery of the self—in a profoundly temporal and historical fashion as the constant theme of religious self-transcendence. He understood such self-transcendence as a creative receptivity and response to God's inscrutable call in the wisdom of creation, in the incarnation, death, and resurrection of Christ, and in the life of every Christian. In the continual quest of self-transcendence of his own life and writing, Merton sketches the importance of both continuity with the past of one's spiritual tradition and openness to the new in the always changing outlines of a symbolic theology of the self.

This theology is the *theologia* of the ancient pattern, one that integrates doctrine and experience and that speaks to the heart as well as to the head. It is a theology of contemplation which is not a record of esoteric experience but rather a creative, literary, and symbolic map of the experience of a single person who—in the gift of re-creation in the written and metaphorical word—continues to speak for many. We discover in his work and in the tangible particularity of one life, the universal dimensions of our own experience.

This symbolic theology makes clear that the universal truth of any religious teaching or doctrine is discovered only in the particularity of historical lives. For the symbols of any religious tradition point beyond themselves to the realm of mystery. In Christian terms, it is both the mystery of the self and the mystery of God. Merton's record of his own experience in exploring the depths of the relationship of self with God is a powerful example of a search for self that is characteristic of our times.

EPILOGUE

Where does this exploration of Merton's developing theology and spirituality of the self lead for contemporary Christians and for other religious seekers? Certainly not to any kind of slavish imitation. Merton would be the last person to say that other people should or could follow his particular route to self-discovery or inner transformation. And he would be the last to say that everyone has a vocation to monastic life or should seek the life of solitude and silence that he wrote about so enthusiastically and so prolifically. But he is clear that the traditions of monasticism and mysticism in which his life was immersed have an important wisdom to offer to anyone about the goals of inner transformation and rebirth that are common to Christianity and to the other religious traditions of the world. These are goals which can be espoused by any person who is serious about going beyond the "approved patterns," the merely conventional responses of any religious system, Christianity included. Merton's life and texts indicate the depth and challenge, the life-long search, entailed in the quest at the heart of all the religions.

For the Christian, Merton's research and analyses raise an issue which lies hidden behind, and perhaps seems to conflict with, much of contemporary theology's focus on the liberation of the oppressed, the needs of the Third World, the care of the poor in any society. It can be described as the theme of individual conversion, or the pursuit of inner transformation, as emphasized by the monastic and mystical traditions. It entails the discovery of the inner self, which is, paradoxically, also a continual re-creation of that self. Merton underscores the importance, indeed the imperative, of continuing the search for the self—that is, the liberation of the true self—even in the midst of intense concern for the problems of the world. His life demonstrates that it may be especially necessary for those who attempt to forge a creative dissent from the established patterns of society to realize that attention to the interior life need not be a privatizing concern. The current turn to questions of spirituality, liturgy, methods of prayer, and routes to personal wholeness is not antithetical to collective and political concerns but is integral to the whole Christian vision. For that whole vision includes the individual and the communal, just as it includes both personal and liturgical prayer, the mystical and the prophetic in its focus on living in the whole Christ.

Merton himself sought to find Christ in the solitude of the monastery and in the writings of monks and mystics whose lives of solitude and contemplation were exemplary for his own life. And at first he believed that his way—the way of withdrawal, contemplation, solitude—was the best way and perhaps the key for everyone. But he came to discover that the way of the monk and mystic meant much more than was immediately apparent. For example, the cultivation of the merely private virtues of obedience, detachment, and humility, in the limited and parochial sense that has been given these virtues by some popular versions of the monastic tradition, fails to encompass the full demands of the Christian spiritual life. These virtues are needed, to be sure, but they are also transformed in Merton's ever-fuller appreciation of what the virtues might mean, of their always fresh possibilities, within the framework of historical experience and the ambiguities of our individual and collective contemporary lives and their sometimes surprising new circumstances. Far from a privatized concern with the self, Merton's life and texts vividly display the personal and the prophetic implications of the virtues in times of change and threat, the risk they require of the Christian.

Another of the ambiguities that this study leads us to ponder is surely the question of a system, pattern, or an approved way in the religious search. Obviously some discipline or system is needed to stabilize the erratic self in its religious search for wholeness, for God. But the system or pattern is meant finally to be left behind. Like the benefits afforded the aspiring musician by years of continual exercises and practice, a religious "system" such as monasticism, or even some personal adaptation of it, gives the practitioner a training which is finally aimed toward release into freedom. In this sense Merton speaks of the monastery as a school not simply of charity, or of humility, but finally of liberty. This school is meant to prepare its students for a kind of standing on their own feet in the liberty which any religious system is meant to produce. Thus the system is transcended. It is a helpful pattern, remains always necessary and never fully dispensable, but is pointed toward something beyond itself.

That goal can be named in many ways. In the texts examined here Merton called it the discovery of the true self. Over the course of his life, however, he continually redescribed the search for this elusive self, using his study of other traditions as well as his own monastic formation and experience to chart the contours of the quest that never ends. His early writings suggest that contemplation of some form will provide the key for everyone. The later texts are clear that there is no key or special way. These texts find in the language of rebirth or transformation a better way to express what is finally inexpressible—the discovery of the self that, in the terms of contemporary theology, is at once the discovery of God. It is a discovery that is a paradox of desire that ceases to desire, an experience that is not an experience, something that God works and so something that *happens* to the one who really lets God operate within. Transformation is given, not achieved. Yet it must be sought.

The early Merton, in his writings on contemplation and mysticism, was prone to a kind of anti-worldliness or anti-materialism, despite his espousal of the sacramentality that is founded in the Christian understanding of the Incarnation. He may have adopted it from his own early conversion experience and from the sharp nature/supernature distinction of the theology of that time, or from Maritain's langauge about the polarity of matter and spirit in the human person. Maritain's insistence that genuine personhood is directed by the spiritual element of the person, not the hateful self or selfish ego of materiality, is a rhetoric that can be oversimplified. Taken together with Merton's love for the apophatic mystical tradition of imageless contemplation, especially John of the Cross's evocation of the imageless darkness that is the goal of the spiritual search, this approach may lead to a skewing of the incarnational and sacramental dimensions that are integral to Christianity.

We can question the goal of an ideal, even an "imageless Christ" sought in prayer, especially in relation to currents of contemporary Christology which emphasize the human life of Jesus as found in the synoptic Gospels, what has been called a Christology "from below." Merton's Christ was the Christ of the more traditional "from above" pattern derived from John's Gospel, a rich pattern to be sure, but one that needs the complementary perspective of the definite images secured in a particular human history, in what can be known of the "Jesus of history." And we can imagine the fruitful consequences for Merton's theology of the self had he been aware of more recent currents of thought about the story of the Jesus of history and his conflicts with religious and political powers.

As Merton explored the meaning of the self, he moved beyond the suggestion of anti-materiality to an affirmation, indeed an embrace, of the world and of the materiality of the human in a genuine and joyous acceptance of the body and its limits and contingencies. He even came to accept the reality of his own dark or negative side and his own death. And he also discovered the continual mistakes and failures that shadow even one who is faithful to the arduous quest, the need for what interpreters Elena Malits and Walter Conn have called "continuing conversion." The texts we have explored chart that persistent search for conversion or transformation in a tough-minded spirituality that does not find a simple path to joyful fulfillment, but must proceed through the experience of monastic or existential dread. Perhaps we share in some way the experience of struggle and dread and despair in our own questions today about governments and the nuclear terror, about the ecological crisis, about the church, about liturgical prayer, in our own wrestling with atheism and unbelief, with the ambiguities of our final religious answers.

Thus, Merton's experience and his study of the world's religious traditions persuaded him that the spiritual life is not a simple affirmation, either of the goodness of the world or of the self that seeks to find itself, to find God. In contrast to some contemporary spiritualities that look for a "quick fix" or an easy way in the human quest for wholeness and the meaning of the self, Merton's life and texts demonstrate how difficult the way to wholeness and to God is, how much is required if one is to be faithful to the wisdom and spirit of the religions of the world. They all commonly maintain that the search is a difficult and life-long process, a mysterious way to which there is no ultimate door or key.

Most importantly, Merton's life and texts reveal his discovery of the necessity of a fundamental and good autonomy as the precondition of the serious spiritual life. Autonomy may seem to be precisely the opposite of the spiritual attitude suggested by the rhetoric of the monks and mystics of Merton's wisdom traditions. They all, Christian and Zen, Sufi and Orthodox, prefer the language of self-denial, self-loss, detachment, obedience, loss of ego in utter dependence on God. Yet here we are reminded of the repeated aphorism of another contemporary theologian, Karl Rahner, about the direct proportion that obtains between autonomy and dependence or closeness to God. Rahner, who characteristically sought to integrate the systematic findings of theology with the experience of the spiritual life, holds that as one comes closer to the authentic autonomy of the self one is, paradoxically, closer and more dependent on God. Further, there is the important insight, reemphasized today in Christian feminist theology, that one cannot give a self which one does not yet fully possess. Merton's discovery of the meaning of authentic autonomy, as the responsible appropriation of the self by the person who is only then capable of self-gift, parallels these recent Christian theological affirmations. Only a self who possesses itself is capable of the austere loss of self about which all the religious traditions speak.

In addition to the important insights which Merton achieved and that mark his work as the most influential and widely read American religious thinker of our time, we must note the weaknesses which his best commentators have pointed out. These criticisms represent the grain of salt with which Merton's writings must always be approached, the critical thought that would avoid a cult of mere adulation and that Merton himself would most appreciate in his readers. It has been said that Merton's spiritual theology is increasingly elitist and eccentric, obsessive and esoteric, and above all, eclectic. And there is some truth to all these claims.

Not everyone has the leisure or the taste for the study and especially for the travel that Merton enjoyed at the beginning and the end of his life and that enriched his understanding of the religions of the world. But we must remember his own comment about *contemplata tradere:* that his vocation requires that he share with others, through his writing, what he has learned. And we can benefit deeply from that sharing. The talent and the almost compulsive need for writing that was both a gift and personal plague for Merton meant that not everything he wrote, with such enthusiasm and fervor, is as carefully honed as the texts examined here. But these texts, at least, as well as some others, can enable his readers to taste the flavor of his finest self-expression. Not everyone can follow Merton's path of continually new exploration into religious traditions beyond one's own. But his work allows the reader to follow and absorb something of the religiously pluralistic world in which we increasingly come to find ourselves and in which our search for God takes place.

Finally, to what extent did Merton remain really Christian? In some of his texts, *The Asian Journal,* for example, there are few references to Jesus Christ that would furnish indisputable evidence of Merton's enduring commitment to Christianity and the monastic path of personal and communal or liturgical prayer he had chosen as a young man. But by putting his texts in the context that his autobiographical writings provide, a context that is richly enhanced by the work of his biographers, it becomes plain that Merton remained deeply Christian to the end. His life work shows us that being Christian today may perhaps require a new kind of openness to the other traditions as well as to the hidden, and surprisingly ecumenical, resources of the monastic and mystical theological traditions of Christianity. Far from an esoteric and unnecessary pursuit, understanding something of the power and the depth of other traditions can lead, beyond old hostilities and beyond superficial comparisons, to a discovery of genuine commonalities and analogies of experience between and among the religions of our world. Such knowledge may be essential if there is to be peace in our increasingly beleaguered world, if we are to be peacemakers in a world torn by conflict. *Zen and the Birds of Appetite,* especially, opens contemporary readers to an intelligent and thoughtful reading of both Christianity and Zen, a reading that is sensitive and nuanced with regard to both the uncanny similarities and the real differences between traditions. Such reading can open one to the hidden dimensions of one's own tradition as well as to the other.

It is not enough simply to read Merton and to live in the world of spirituality his writing can create. Rather, it is necessary to follow his path, not in simple imitation of course, but in the creative and finally transforming religious quest that is the search for the self and for God in our time. Merton's spiritual theology of the self provides for our individual and communal lives a healthy and intelligent corrective to any suggestion that the way to wisdom and spirit is simple, or easy, or smooth. As Chris-

tianity teaches, and the other religions of the world as well, it is
an arduous path, riddled with many pitfalls. Among these snares
are the blindnesses and errors created by the neurotic, self-
deceptive, false, or merely external self. Merton's life and texts
warn of the dangers along the way at the same time as they encourage us to start out on the road of self-discovery. It is a journey that can lead us, beyond and often despite ourselves, to the
discovery of the presence of God in our own tangled lives.

NOTES

Introduction

1. Cf. e.g., Christopher Lasch, *The Culture of Narcissism: American Life in an Age of Diminishing Expectations* (New York: W. W. Norton, 1979); Robert N. Bellah and others, *Habits of the Heart: Individualism and Commitment in American Life* (Berkeley: University of California Press, 1985).

2. Cf. Raymond Bailey, *Thomas Merton on Mysticism* (New York: Doubleday, 1976), 205; John J. Higgins, S.J., *Thomas Merton on Prayer* (Garden City, N.Y.: Doubleday, 1973), 58–64; James Finley, *Merton's Palace of Nowhere: A Search for God through Awareness of the True Self* (Notre Dame, Ind.: Ave Maria Press, 1978); William H. Shannon, *Thomas Merton's Dark Path: The Inner Experience of a Contemplative* (New York: Farrar, Straus & Giroux: 1981). The latter two books touch on some of the same themes as the present study, but neither places them in an autobiographical framework that shows the development of Merton's thought.

3. Merton ranked his one attempt at writing theology, *The Ascent to Truth* (New York: Harcourt, Brace, 1951) as only "fair" among his many books, and once remarked that although he wished he had studied theology with more of the sharpness and precision of the Dominicans, he had some difficulty with their distinctions which, like their traditional colors, were black and white. Cf. Bailey, *Mysticism*, 255–256, n. 14 and Merton, *The Sign of Jonas* (Garden City, N.Y.: Doubleday, 1953), 208. On Merton's struggle with the thought of Thomas Aquinas, see Bailey, 106 ff., and on his deep admiration for

Aquinas, see Merton, *Conjectures of a Guilty Bystander* (Garden City, N.Y.: paperback edition, Doubleday, 1966), 203–208.

4. Merton's specifically autobiographical writings include *The Seven Storey Mountain* (New York: Harcourt, Brace, 1948); *The Sign of Jonas,* 1953; *The Secular Journal* (New York: McGraw-Hill, 1959); *Conjectures of a Guilty Bystander,* 1966; *My Argument with the Gestapo: A Macaronic Journal* (Garden City, N.Y.: Doubleday, 1969); *The Asian Journal* (New York: New Directions, 1973). On Merton's influence see Hal Bridges, *American Mysticism* (New York: Harper & Row, 1970), 65–72, and Walter Capps, *Hope Against Hope* (Philadelphia: Fortress, 1976), 105–129, 147–167. On the relation between life story and theology, see James McClendon, *Biography as Theology* (Nashville: Abingdon, 1974).

5. *Cistercian Fathers,* vol. XX: *Collected Essays,* 55. The twenty-four volumes of *Collected Essays* contain both published and unpublished writings of Merton and are housed in the Thomas Merton Studies Center at Bellarmine College, Louisville.

6. For Merton's own understanding of "connaturality" see *Ascent to Truth,* 274–287. On the symbolic character of autobiography, see James Olney, *Metaphors of Self: The Meaning of Autobiography* (Princeton: Princeton University Press, 1972). Cf. Merton's *Secular Journal,* 24: "The logic of the poet—that is, the logic of language or the experience itself—develops the way an organism grows: it spreads out toward what it loves, and is heliotropic, like a plant. A tree grows out into a free form. It is never ideal, only free; never typical, always individual." Elena Malits' *The Solitary Explorer: Thomas Merton's Transforming Journey* (San Francisco: Harper & Row, 1980) is especially suggestive in its discussion of Merton's use of metaphor and symbol.

7. *Conjectures of a Guilty Bystander,* 194; cf. also Merton, *Mystics and Zen Masters* (New York: Dell, 1967), 212–213. For a contemporary interpretation of *theologia,* see Edward Farley, *Theologia: The Fragmentation and Unity of Theological Education,* (Philadelphia: Fortress, 1983), 29–48.

8. See Elena Malits, "Thomas Merton: Symbol and Synthesis of Contemporary Catholicism," *Critic* 35, no. 3 (Spring 1977), 26–33.

9. *Cistercian Studies* 18, nos. 1–4 (1983) and 19, nos. 1–4 (1984).

10. Edward Rice, *The Man in the Sycamore Tree: The Good Life and Hard Times of Thomas Merton* (Garden City, N.Y.: Doubleday, 1970); Monica Furlong, *Merton: A Biography* (San Francisco: Harper & Row, 1980); Michael Mott, *The Seven Mountains of Thomas Merton* (Boston: Houghton, Mifflin, 1984).

1. Seeds of the Self

1. Merton places his own life into periods and gives a critical assessment of his writing of each period in his "Preface" to *A Thomas Merton Reader,* ed. Thomas P. McDonnell (Garden City, N.Y.: Doubleday, rev. ed., 1974).

2. Rice, 55. For the dates of the writing of *The Seven Storey Mountain,* see Peter Kountz, "The Seven Storey Mountain of Thomas Merton," *Thought* 49 (September 1974), 252.

3. *Seeds of Contemplation* (Norfolk, Conn.: New Directions, 1949), 14, 13.

4. Ibid., 17–21.

5. Ibid., 22–23, 26; see also 63.

6. Ibid., 26.

7. Ibid., 27.

8. *The Seven Storey Mountain,* 11.

9. *Seeds of Contemplation,* 28.

10. Ibid., 29.

11. Ibid., 31. The word *experimental* as used here reflects an older usage, common before the advent of experimental science. It means "experiential" as a personal realization of the presence of God in creation and in more actual fashion, in grace.

12. *The Waters of Siloe* (New York: Harcourt, Brace, 1949), 366.

13. *Seeds of Contemplation,* 31–32; in the 1961 revision, Merton removed the reference to the "mystics of the Orient."

14. Ibid.

15. Ibid., 33.

16. Ibid., 34, 37.

17. Mott, 209.

18. Cf. Thomas Merton, "Nature and Art in William Blake: An

Essay in Interpretation" (1939), Appendix 1 in *The Literary Essays of Thomas Merton,* ed. Brother Patrick Hart (New York: New Directions, 1981), 387–453.

19. *Seeds of Contemplation,* 65, 67.

20. Ibid., 67–69. Merton's aversion to system and technique in contrast to experience in the contemplative life is enduring. Cf., e.g., *Mystics and Zen Masters,* 41, 220.

21. *Seeds of Contemplation,* 38–42.

22. Ibid., 46–49. Obscurity and darkness are pervasive themes in Merton's spiritual writing; cf. John F. Teahan, "A Dark and Empty Way: Thomas Merton and the Apophatic Tradition," *Journal of Religion* 58, no. 3 (July 1978), 263–287.

23. *The Seven Storey Mountain,* 61.

24. *The Sign of Jonas,* 246–247.

25. Kountz, 265.

26. *Seeds of Contemplation,* 57–60.

27. Ibid., 51.

28. Ibid., 152–154.

29. Ibid., 164–169, 165, 186.

30. Ibid., 194–196.

31. Ibid., 196, 198. On Merton's successive attempts at "self-loss" in his writing, see Thomas M. King, "The Writer Loses Himself: A Study of Thomas Merton," *Chicago Studies* 24, no. 1 (April 1985), 69–85.

32. *The Sign of Jonas,* 166, 201.

33. "Preface, *New Seeds of Contemplation* (New York: New Directions, 1962), ix–x.

34. See, e.g., *Seeds of Contemplation,* 173.

35. Jacques Maritain, *Scholasticism and Politics,* trans. Mortimer Adler (Garden City, N.Y.: Doubleday Image Books, 1960, first published Macmillan Co., 1940), 63.

36. Ibid., 66, 64.

37. Ibid., 67.

38. Ibid., 68.

39. Ibid., 69.

40. Ibid.

41. *New Seeds of Contemplation,* 1–5, 290–297. Cf. Donald Gray-

ston, "The Making of a Spiritual Classic: Thomas Merton's *Seeds of Contemplation* and *New Seeds of Contemplation*" *Studies in Religion* 3 (1974), 339– 356, who indicates that there was another revision of the book in the same year as the original edition. Grayston analyzes the differences in the editions, including one telling sentence which is already omitted by the end of 1949: "For outside the *magisterium* directly guided by the Spirit of God we find no such contemplation and no such union with Him—only the void of nirvana or the feeble intellectual light of Platonic idealism, or the sensual dreams of the Sufis" (87). Grayston's full research on altogether five versions of *Seeds of Contemplation,* including the original typescript and *New Seeds,* is found in his book *Thomas Merton: The Making of a Spiritual Theologian* (New York and Toronto: Edwin Mellen Press, 1985).

42. *New Seeds of Contemplation,* 6–8.

43. Ibid., 8–10. Merton often uses Descartes's *cogito* as a shorthand phrase to refer to the objectifying character of modern consciousness; cf. *Conjectures of a Guilty Bystander,* 181, 265, 285; *Zen and the Birds of Appetite* (New York: New Directions, 1968), 22–28.

44. *New Seeds of Contemplation,* 9–13.

45. Ibid., 290–297.

2. Seeking the Spirit: The Christian Inheritance

1. *The Silent Life* (New York: Farrar, Straus & Giroux, 1957); "The Inner Experience" is a manuscript of which there are four versions in the collection at the Thomas Merton Studies Center at Bellarmine College, Louisville. It was begun in 1959. Merton finished the fourth draft shortly before he left for Asia in 1968 but had left instructions that it was not to be published as a book. It is that draft that is used for reference here. Portions of the manuscript were recently selected and edited by Brother Patrick Hart for a series of eight articles in *Cistercian Studies,* vols. 18 and 19. Cf. Bailey, 265, n. 88; 157–210. William H. Shannon, in *Thomas Merton's Dark Path* presents an overview of "The Inner Experience" and offers a selection of texts from the work as well. There are brief references to the theme of the self in other Merton books of this period: *No Man Is an Island* (New York: Har-

court, Brace, 1955), 34–35; *The Wisdom of the Desert* (New York: New Directions, 1960), 5–8; *Life and Holiness* (New York: Herder and Herder, 1961), 50.

2. "Preface," *A Thomas Merton Reader,* 15–16.

3. Rice, 76.

4. *The Sign of Jonas,* 317–318.

5. Rice, 76–81; Mott, 278–283; Dennis Q. McInerny, *Thomas Merton: The Man and His Work,* Cistercian Studies Series no. 27 (Washington, D.C.: Consortium, 1974), 49; Thérèse Lentfoehr, "The Spiritual Writer," in *Thomas Merton, Monk: A Monastic Tribute,* ed. Patrick Hart (New York: Sheed and Ward, 1974), 117–118. See also Merton's "Philosophy of Solitude," *Disputed Questions* (New York: Farrar, Straus & Giroux, 1960), 163–193; *The Monastic Journey,* ed. Patrick Hart (Kansas City: Sheed, Andrews, McMeel, 1977) 135–143; 151–162.

6. *The Silent Life,* viii–xiv. Cf. *Waters of Siloe,* 16–17; *Monastic Journey,* 144–150.

7. *The Silent Life,* 1–4.

8. Ibid., 4–10.

9. Furlong, 56–62.

10. Cf. Cassian, *Conferences* 1, vii, Migne, P.L. 49: 489, as cited in *The Silent Life,* 11.

11. *The Silent Life,* 11–20; cf. *Monastic Journey,* 90–94.

12. *The Silent Life,* 21–23; cf. *Waters of Siloe,* 57–59.

13. *The Silent Life,* 23–25. Merton's characteristic expression is Bernard's "school of charity"; see *Waters of Siloe,* 57 and 365.

14. The initial manuscript of "The Inner Experience" is called "The Dark Path." The first several chapters are nearly completed and remain essentially unchanged through the several revisions. It is in these chapters that the theme of the self is most fully developed. See the selected texts in William Shannon, *Thomas Merton's Dark Path,* 114–141, and the articles in *Cistercian Studies,* vols. 18 and 19.

15. "The Inner Experience" (fourth draft), 2–5.

16. Ibid., 4–6; 30; cf. *The Asian Journal,* 116, 154.

17. "The Inner Experience," 6–8.

18. Ibid., 8. Cf. D. T. Suzuki, *Zen Buddhism,* ed. William Barrett (Garden City, N.Y.: Doubleday Anchor, 1956), 106–107.

19. "The Inner Experience," 9–10.

20. Ibid., 11; Merton refers to Augustine on the distinction between the inmost self and God in the *Confessions,* 7, 16.

21. "The Inner Experience," 11.

22. Ibid., 11–16.

23. Ibid., 16; see Shannon, 120.

24. "The Inner Experience," 16.

25. Ibid., 17–19. On the concrete intuition, without affirmation or negation, see *The Asian Journal,* 137, 233 ff.

26. "The Inner Experience," 19–22.

27. Ibid., 22; cf. Bailey, 100–101 on Merton's knowledge of Freud and Jung and his abiding interest in psychology.

28. "The Inner Experience," 22–23.

29. Ibid., 23–26.

30. Ibid., 27–32.

31. Ibid., 32–35.

32. Ibid., 36–43.

33. Ibid., 48–52.

34. Ibid., 52–53.

35. Bailey, 100–101; on the "shadow" or the "dark self" see, for example, Carl G. Jung, *Psychology and Religion* (New Haven and London: Yale University Press, 1938), 93–95; Jung, *Man and His Symbols* (New York: Dell, 1964), 73 ff.

3. Conjectures at a Turning Point

1. Mott, 435–454. Merton's love poems have recently been published as *Eighteen Poems* (New York: New Directions, 1986).

2. Rice, 79. See also James Thomas Baker, *Thomas Merton: Social Critic* (Lexington: University of Kentucky Press, 1971).

3. Mott, 289–299.

4. *Behavior of Titans* (New York: New Directions, 1961), 51–64; see also Merton's *Seeds of Destruction* (New York: Farrar, Straus & Giroux, 1964) and *Gandhi on Non-Violence* (New York: New Directions, 1964).

5. *Conjectures of a Guilty Bystander,* 6, 19: see also 56 and 91 on

Merton's understanding of individualism and collectivism as opposed to personalism.

6. Ibid., 137.

7. Ibid., 156–157.

8. Mott, 313.

9. Michael Mott, Author's Response in "Review Symposium," *Horizons* 12:1 (Spring 1985), 158.

10. "Hagia Sophia," *Emblems of a Season of Fury* (New York: New Directions, 1963), 62.

11. *Conjectures of a Guilty Bystander,* 158.

12. Ibid., 14–15. Cf. *Waters of Siloe,* 67–83 for the early Merton's interpretation of De Rancé's seventeenth-century reform of LaTrappe, a chapter in Cistercian history when the doors and windows of freedom were locked in a rigid and rigorous discipline.

13. *Conjectures of a Guilty Bystander,* 20–21.

14. Ibid., 25. There is a small group of interesting letters from Merton to Ananda Coomaraswamy's widow, Dona Luisa, in the collection of Merton's letters selected and edited by William H. Shannon called *The Hidden Ground of Love* (New York: Farrar, Straus & Giroux, 1985), 125–133.

15. *Conjectures of a Guilty Bystander,* 81–83. Merton's "humanism" or "personalism" is rooted in the classic doctrine of the Incarnation; cf. *Disputed Questions,* 97–126, 127–148; *Mystics and Zen Masters,* 113–127; Bailey, 151–157.

16. "The Pasternak Affair," *Disputed Questions,* 12–14.

17. Ibid., 18.

18. *Conjectures of a Guilty Bystander,* 146; see also 245, 264. Cf. Dietrich Bonhoeffer, *Letters and Papers from Prison,* ed. Eberhard Bethge, trans. Reginald H. Fuller (New York: Macmillan, 1953), 194–198.

19. *Conjectures of a Guilty Bystander,* 189, 262; cf. 177.

20. Ibid., 113, 154.

21. Ibid., 150.

22. Ibid., 184.

23. Ibid., 224; see also 113–114.

24. Ibid., 225; cf. Merton's later comment in *The Asian Journal,* 90: "What is important is not liberation from the body but liberation

from the mind. We are not entangled in our own body but entangled in our own mind."

25. *Conjectures of a Guilty Bystander*, 225.

26. Ibid., 226.

27. Ibid., 33–39 on the "American myth" and 257 on Merton's new affirmation of the goodness of the world. The theme of cosmic, created, natural goodness is central in Merton's *Raids on the Unspeakable* (New York: New Directions, 1964), especially in the sketches "Rain and the Rhinoceros," "Prometheus," "Atlas and the Fatman," and "Atlas Watches." Atlas, Merton says, "is precisely the world *as good*" (5).

28. *Conjectures of a Guilty Bystander*, 264–267.

29. Ibid., 266.

30. Ibid., 268.

31. Ibid., 131–132, 151. Merton attributes the notion of the *point vierge* of the spirit to Louis Massignon's *Mardis de Dar-es-Salam*. It recurs in *The Asian Journal* as *temps vierge*, 117: "The contemplative life must provide an area, a space of liberty, of silence, in which possibilities are allowed to surface and new choices—become manifest. It should create a new experience of time, not as stopgap, stillness, but as "temps vierge"—not a blank to be filled or an untouched space to be conquered and violated, but a space which can enjoy its own potentialities and hope—and its own presence to itself. One's *own* time. But not dominated by one's ego and its demands. Hence open to others—*compassionate* time, rooted in the sense of common illusion and in criticism of it."

32. *Conjectures of a Guilty Bystander*, 158.

33. Ibid., 11. On Merton's view of the "sapiential" in contrast to the "scientific" spirit, see *Mystics and Zen Masters*, 203–214.

34. *Conjectures of a Guilty Bystander*, 291–292. Cf. *The Asian Journal*, 238: "Suddenly there is a point where religion becomes laughable. Then you decide that you are nevertheless religious."

35. *Conjectures of a Guilty Bystander*, 282, 221. And in the *Asian Journal*, 91: "The highest of vows . . . is that in which there is no longer anything to be accomplished. Nothing is vowed. No one vows it." And 169, where Merton quotes Pierre Emmanuel: ". . . to conceive the call of God as an expressed order to carry out a task certainly

is not always false, but it is only true after a long interior struggle in which it becomes obvious that no such constraint is apparent. It also happens that the order comes to maturity along with the one who must carry it out and that it becomes in some way this very being, who has now arrived at full maturity."

36. *Conjectures of a Guilty Bystander*, 245.

4. *The Wisdom of the Self: Learning from the East*

1. Rice, 86–91: see also Merton's *Faith and Violence* (Notre Dame, Ind.: University of Notre Dame Press, 1968).

2. "Day of a Stranger," *A Thomas Merton Reader*, 431–432. For the context of the writing of this essay, see Lentfoehr, 118.

3. "Day of a Stranger," 432–433.

4. Ibid., 434.

5. Ibid., 435–436. Cf. Lentfoehr, 118, where Merton is quoted: "The 'I' that goes from day to day is not an important 'I' and his future matters little. And the deeper 'I' is in an eternal present. If a door should one day open from one realm to the other, the 'I' (whoever that is!) will be glad of it" (letter dated September 17, 1965).

6. "Day of a Stranger," 437.

7. Ibid.

8. Merton, *Mystics and Zen Masters*, 12–18, especially 17–18.

9. Thomas Merton, *The Way of Chuang Tzu* (New York: New Directions, 1965), 15–16, 11, 23–27.

10. *Zen and the Birds of Appetite*, 8, 35, 42–45.

11. Ibid., 45.

12. Ibid., 49.

13. *Zen and the Birds of Appetite*, 49–50. Cf. also 139–140: "True, they both [linguistic analysis and Zen] reject mystifications and ideo-logical superstructures which, in attempting to account for what is in front of us, get in its way. But I, for one, completely agree with Herbert Marcuse's analysis of the 'one-dimensional thinking' in which the very rationality and exactitude of technological society and its various jus-tifications, add up to one more total mystification." For examples of Merton's use of anti-logic and anti-language, see his *Cables to the Ace*

or Familiar Liturgies of Misunderstanding (New York: New Directions, 1968) and with Robert Lax, *A Catch of Anti-Letters* (Kansas City, Mo.: Sheed, Andrews and McMeel, 1978).

14. Ibid., 53–54.
15. Ibid., 51.
16. Ibid., 55.
17. Ibid., 55–57.
18. Ibid., 9–12; 99–138.
19. Ibid., 12.
20. Ibid.; Appendix VII, "Marxism and Monastic Perspectives," *The Asian Journal,* 338. For this understanding of "post-conventional autonomy" see Lawrence Kohlberg, *The Philosophy of Moral Development: Moral Stages and the Idea of Justice* (San Francisco: Harper & Row, 1981) and *The Psychology of Moral Development and Validity of Moral Stages* (San Francisco: Harper & Row, 1984). See also James W. Fowler, *Stages of Faith: The Psychology of Human Development and the Quest for Meaning* (San Francisco: Harper & Row, 1981 and Robert Kegan, *The Evolving Self: Problems and Process in Human Development* (Cambridge: Harvard University Press, 1982).

21. Cf. Walter E. Conn, "Merton's 'True Self': Moral Autonomy and Religious Conversion," *Journal of Religion* 65 no. 4 (October 1985), 513–529. The two final chapters of Conn's book, *Christian Conversion: A Developmental Interpretation of Autonomy and Surrender* (New York: Paulist, 1986), 158–268 examine in detail Merton's conversion experiences in light of moral stage theory.

22. *Zen and the Birds of Appetite,* 71.
23. Ibid., 72.
24. Ibid., 73–74. Cf. *The Asian Journal,* 154: "The door of emptiness. Of no-where. Of no place for a self, which cannot be entered by a self. And therefore is of no use to someone who is going somewhere. Is it a door at all? The door of no-door." See R. J. Zwi Werblowsky, "On the Mystical Rejection of Mystical Illuminations: A Note on St. John of the Cross," *Religous Studies* 1 (1965–66), 177–184.

25. *Zen and the Birds of Appetite,* 74–75.
26. Ibid., 76. Cf. "The Inner Experience," 11; *The Asian Journal,* 154: "The door without wish. The undesired. The unplanned door.

The door never expected. Never wanted. Not desirable as a door. Not a joke. Not a trap door. Not select. Not exclusive. Not for a few. Nor for many. Not *for*. Door without aim. Door without end. Does not respond to a key—so do not imagine you have a key. . . . Christ said, 'I am the door.' The nailed door. The cross. . . . The resurrection: 'You see, I am *not* a door. . . . ' 'I am the Light,' and the light is in the world from the beginning."

27. *Zen and the Birds of Appetite*, 76–78.

28. Ibid., 15–21.

29. Ibid., 22.

30. Ibid., 23–24.

31. See Karl Rahner, "Experience of Self and Experience of God," *Theological Investigations* 13 (New York: Seabury, 1975), 122–132. The mystical sources of Rahner's perspective are analyzed in Klaus P. Fischer, *Der Mensch als Geheimnis* (Freiburg: Herder, 1974).

32. *Zen and the Birds of Appetite*, 30.

33. Ibid., 30–31.

34. Ibid., 31.

5. "I Live Now Not I . . . "

1. *The Asian Journal*, "Foreword" by Brother Patrick Hart, xxi–xxix, and Appendix VII: "Marxism and Monastic Perspectives," 326–343.

2. *Contemplation in a World of Action* (Garden City, N.Y.: Doubleday, 1971), 58–59. On the importance of dialogue in relation to the monastic tradition, see Merton's "Contemplation and Dialogue," *Mystics and Zen Masters*, 203–214.

3. *Contemplation in a World of Action*, 63.

4. Ibid., 68.

5. Ibid., 70–71.

6. Ibid., 75–76. For a moving example of Merton's love of nature and the sacramental significance that nature bears, see his "Rain and the Rhinoceros," in *Raids on the Unspeakable*, 9–23.

7. *Contemplation in a World of Action*, 207. See also Merton's essays, "Zen Buddhist Monasticism," and "The Zen Koan," *Mystics and*

Zen Masters, 215–254. On the "rebirth" or "transformation" that is common to the religious traditions, see Merton's comment on monasticism in *The Asian Journal,* 340: "What is essential in the monastic life is not embedded in buildings, is not embedded in clothing, is not necessarily embedded even in a rule. It is concerned with this business of total inner transformation. All other things serve that end."

8. *Contemplation in a World of Action,* 208–209. For analysis of Merton's thought on creative dissent, see the two studies of Merton's social criticism: Baker, *Thomas Merton: Social Critic,* and David W. Givey, *The Social Thought of Thomas Merton* (Chicago: Franciscan Herald Press, 1983).

9. *Contemplation in a World of Action,* 211. See the letters of Merton to Reza Arasteh in Shannon, *The Hidden Ground of Love,* 40–43.

10. *Contemplation in a World of Action,* 212.

11. Ibid., 213. Cf. Furlong, 218–235; Mott, 273.

12. Ibid., 214–215.

13. Ibid., 216. On the eschatological theme, see Merton's *Raids on the Unspeakable,* especially "The Time of the End Is the Time of No Room," 65–75.

14. *Contemplation in a World of Action,* 216–217.

15. *Contemplative Prayer* (Garden City, N.Y.: Doubleday Image, 1971); *The Climate of Monastic Prayer* (Washington, D.C.: Cistercian Publications, Consortium Press, 1973).

16. *Contemplative Prayer,* 20–26, 24. On the ancient prayer of the heart, see Merton's study "Russian Mystics," *Mystics and Zen Masters,* 178–192. On existentialism, see "The Other Side of Despair: Notes on Christian Existentialism," ibid., 255–280.

17. *Contemplative Prayer,* 24.

18. Ibid., 27.

19. Ibid., 38–40. Merton's suspicion about "approved patterns" is life-long. See *Seeds of Contemplation,* 67–69.

20. *Contemplative Prayer,* 43.

21. Ibid., 59–61.

22. Ibid., 68.

23. Ibid. Note the contrast with Merton's earlier statement about created identity in *Seeds of Contemplation,* 27.

24. *Contemplative Prayer,* 70.

25. Ibid., 76.

26. Ibid., 79-83, 88.

27. Ibid., 96. See *Conjectures of a Guilty Bystander*, 170: "consider the ambiguities of 'doing good,' knowing that when one is firmly convinced of his own rightness and goodness, he can without qualm perpetrate the most appalling evil. After all, it was the righteous, the holy, the 'believers in God' who crucified Christ, and they did so in the name of righteousness, holiness, and even of God (John 10: 32)."

28. *Contemplative Prayer*, 97.

29. Ibid., 98.

30. Ibid., 98-99.

31. Ibid., 101. On Merton's appropriation of Heidegger's thought, see *Conjectures of a Guilty Bystander*, 232-233; for his interesting comparison of Sartre with St. Anselm, ibid., 327-330; and for his reflections on Kierkegaard and Protestant existentialism, ibid., 170.

32. *Contemplative Prayer*, 102.

33. Ibid., 103-104.

34. Ibid., 106.

35. Ibid., 107-113. On Merton's understanding of Marx and Marxism, see Baker, 26, 67-72, 130-131.

36. *Contemplative Prayer*, 113.

6. *The Story of the Self*

1. See, for example, *Zen and the Birds of Appetite*, 71, where Merton refers to the "transcendent Self" which is "metaphysically distinct from the Self of God and yet perfectly identified with that Self by love and freedom, so that there appears to be but one Self." And ibid., 86-87, where, in comparing Christian love and Buddhist compassion, he writes: "Such love is beyond desire and beyond all restrictions of a desiring and self-centered self. Such love begins only when the ego renounces its claim to absolute autonomy and ceases to live in a little kingdom of desires in which it is its own end and reason for existing. . . . In either case [Christianity or Buddhism] the highest illumination of love is an explosion of the power of Love's evidence in which all

the psychological limits of an 'experiencing' subject are dissolved and what remains is the transcendent clarity of love itself, realized in the ego-less subject in a mystery beyond comprehension but not beyond consent."

2. "Is the World a Problem?" *Commonweal* 84 (June 3, 1966), 305.

3. Conn, "Merton's 'True Self': Moral Autonomy and Religious Conversion," 527–529, and *Christian Conversion,* 263–268; King, "The Writer Loses Himself," 69–85.

4. *The Asian Journal,* 143.

5. Ibid., 233–236.

6. See, e.g., Sigmund Freud, *An Outline of Psychoanalysis,* trans. James Strachey (New York: W. W. Norton, 1949).

7. See Jung, *Psychology and Religion* and *Man and His Symbols;* Erik Erikson, *Childhood and Society* (New York: W. W. Norton, 1963) and *Identity: Youth and Crisis* (New York: W. W. Norton, 1968).

8. "Theology of Creativity," *The Literary Essays of Thomas Merton,* 370.

9. See the discussions of autobiography and the self in Karl J. Weintraub, "Autobiography and Historical Consciousness," *Critical Inquiry* 1, no. 4 (June 1975), 821–848, and Weintraub, *The Value of the Individual: Self and Circumstance in Autobiography* (Chicago: University of Chicago, 1978); Olney, *Metaphors of Self: The Meaning of Autobiography;* Roy Pascal, *Design and Truth in Autobiography* (London: Routledge & Kegan Paul, 1960); John Norris, *Versions of the Self* (Berkeley: University of California, 1966); Stephen Crites, "The Narrative Quality of Experience," *Journal of the American Academy of Religion* 39, no. 3 (September 1971), 291–311.

10. In addition to *Zen and the Birds of Appetite,* see *Mystics and Zen Masters,* 215–254.

11. *The Asian Journal,* 311.

12. *Contemplation in a World of Action,* 352. See Elena Malits' insightful interpretation of Merton's metaphors in this and other passages in "Thomas Merton and the Possibilities of Religious Imagination," *The Message of Thomas Merton,* ed. Brother Patrick Hart (Kalamazoo, Mich.: Cistercian Publications, 1981), 42–54.

SELECTED BIBLIOGRAPHY OF BOOKS BY THOMAS MERTON

The Ascent to Truth. New York: Harcourt, Brace, 1951.

The Asian Journal of Thomas Merton. Edited by Naomi Burton, Brother Patrick Hart, and James Laughlin, New York: New Directions, 1973.

Bread in the Wilderness. New York: New Directions, 1952.

Cables to the Ace: Or Familiar Liturgies of Misunderstanding. New York: New Directions, 1968.

The Climate of Monastic Prayer. Spencer, Mass: Cistercian Publications, 1969 (second edition under the title *Contemplative Prayer*, see below).

Conjectures of a Guilty Bystander. Garden City, N.Y.: Doubleday, 1966.

Contemplative Prayer. Garden City, N.Y.: Doubleday, 1969.

Contemplation in a World of Action. Garden City, N.Y.: Doubleday, 1971.

Disputed Questions. New York: Farrar, Straus & Cudahy, 1960.

Emblems of a Season of Fury. Norfolk, Conn.: New Directions, 1963.

Faith and Violence: Christian Teaching and Christian Practice. Notre Dame, Ind.: University of Notre Dame Press, 1968.

Figures for an Apocalypse. Norfolk, Conn.: New Directions, 1947.

The Geography of Lograire. New York: New Directions, 1969.

Hagia Sophia. Lexington, Ky.: Stamperia del Santuccio, 1962.

Life and Holiness. Garden City, N.Y.: Doubleday, 1964.

The Living Bread. New York: Farrar, Straus & Cudahy, 1956.

The Monastic Journey. Edited by Brother Patrick Hart. New York: Doubleday Image, 1978.

My Argument with the Gestapo: A Macaronic Journal. Garden City, N.Y.: Doubleday, 1969.

Mystics and Zen Masters. New York: Farrar, Straus & Giroux, 1967.

The New Man. New York: Mentor-Omega Books, 1961.

New Seeds of Contemplation. Norfolk, Conn.: New Directions, 1961.

No Man Is an Island. Garden City, N.Y.: Doubleday, 1967.

The Non-Violent Alternative. Edited and with an introduction by Gordon C. Zahn. New York: Farrar, Straus, & Giroux, 1980.

Original Child Bomb: Points for Meditation to be scratched on the walls of a cave. New York: New Directions, 1962.

Praying the Psalms. Collegeville, Minn.: Liturgical Press, 1956.

Raids on the Unspeakable. New York: New Directions, 1966.

Seasons of Celebration. New York: Farrar, Straus & Giroux, 1965.

The Secular Journal of Thomas Merton. Garden City, N.Y.: Doubleday, 1969.

Seeds of Contemplation. Norfolk, Conn.: New Directions, 1949.

Seeds of Destruction. New York: Farrar, Straus & Giroux, 1964.

Selected Poems. New York: New Directions, 1959.

The Seven Storey Mountain. New York: Harcourt, Brace, 1948.

The Sign of Jonas. Garden City, N.Y.: Doubleday, 1956.

The Silent Life. New York: Farrar, Straus & Cudahy, 1957.

The Solitary Life. Lexington, Ky.: Stamperia del Santuccio, 1960.

Spiritual Direction and Meditation. Collegeville, Minn.: Liturgical Press, 1960.

The Strange Islands. New York: New Directions, 1957.

The Tears of the Blind Lions. New York: New Directions, 1949.

Thoughts in Solitude. Garden City, N.Y.: Doubleday, 1968.

Thomas Merton on Peace. Edited and with an Introduction by Gordon C. Zahn. New York: McCall, 1971.

A Thomas Merton Reader. Edited by Thomas P. McDonnell. New York: Harcourt, Brace and World, 1962.

The Waters of Siloe. New York: Harcourt, Brace, 1949.

The Way of Chuang Tzu. New York: New Directions, 1965.

What Is Contemplation? London: Burns, Oates and Washbourne, 1950.

The Wisdom of the Desert. New York: New Directions, 1960.

Zen and the Birds of Appetite. New York: New Directions, 1968.

INDEX

Anatta: Buddhist no-self, 42, 83; apophatic tradition, 19

Aquinas, Thomas, 14, 18, 27, 70, 87, 91, 105

Arasteh, Reza, 103, 104

Art as virtue, 18

Art and Scholasticism, 18. *See also* Maritain, Jacques

The Ascent to Truth, 78

Asceticism, 37, 39, 42, 46, 53, 60, 64, 98, 100, 110, 112, 114

The Asian Journal, 97, 127-128, 136, 139, 147

Augustine of Hippo, 12, 14, 76, 130

Autonomy, 32-33, 64-65, 67, 71-72, 84-85, 99-100, 114, 122, 124-125, 127-128, 135, 137, 145-146

Bangkok, 97

Baptism, 16, 17, 50, 53, 117

Barth, Karl, 55, 63, 69

Behavior of Titans, 56

Being, 68, 70, 71

Benedict, St., 96, 105, 112

Benedictine tradition, 112

Bernard of Clairvaux, 11, 15, 48

Berrigan, Daniel, 75

Bhagavad Gita, 48

Bible, 4, 35, 82, 108

Blake, William, 18, 27

Bonhoeffer, Dietrich, 55, 62

Buddha, 70, 83, 88, 127.

Buddhism, *See* Zen.

Camus, Albert, 138

Capitalism, 107

Cassian, 38, 83

Chao-pien, 43, 45

Christ, 8, 32, 49, 53, 61-62, 68, 72, 79, 82-83, 84, 86-89 93, 98, 102, 106-107, 111, 113-115, 122, 129, 132, 133, 139-140, 142, 144, 147

Chuang Tsu, 76, 79

Church, 4, 47, 106, 107, 117, 119, 137, 145

Church fathers, 26, 35, 96, 121, 131

Cistercians, 10, 15, 17, 56, 78, 94. *See also* Trappist

The Climate of Monastic Prayer, 107

Columbia University, 18, 60, 67, 76, 97

Confucianism, 107

Conjectures of a Guilty Bystander, 7, 8, 54-72, 75, 134, 135

Conn, Walter, 144

The Constitution on the Church in the Modern World, 54

167

Contemplation, 2, 5-6, 10-11, 15-16, 20-21, 24-26, 31-33, 36, 40-41, 48-50, 52-54, 69, 72-74, 76, 78, 87, 92-93, 96, 98, 108, 112, 118, 120, 122-123, 129, 134, 136-138, 140, 142-144

Contemplation in a World of Action, 8, 96, 97-107, 136-138

Contemplative Prayer, 8, 96, 97, 107-120, 136, 138

Coomaraswamy, Ananda, 60

Creation, 15, 26, 32, 66, 71, 73-74, 87, 101, 111, 122, 126, 127, 129, 131-132, 134, 140

Cross, 83, 93

Dalai Lama, 94

Dark night. *See* Dread

Dark self, 52, 72, 127, 128, 133

Darwin, Charles, 99

Day, Dorothy, 75

"Day of a Stranger," 76-78, 135

De Rancé, 17th c. Abbot of La Trappe, 17

Descartes, René, 31, 67, 90

Desert fathers, 96, 108

Dr. Zhivago (Pasternak), 61, 62, 134

Dread, existential or monastic, 108-120, 121, 126, 129, 131, 138, 145

Eastern Christianity, 5, 26, 49, 79, 89, 116; Greek Orthodoxy, 53, 79, 107, 145; Cappadocian and Alexandrian fathers, 90

Eastern religions, 15, 55, 74, 76, 94

Eckhart, Meister, 83-84, 90, 96

Ego, 2, 15, 18, 28, 40-41, 67-68, 72-73, 81-82, 84, 86-90, 93, 103-104, 115, 123-126, 128, 130, 136, 144-145

Erikson, Erik, 128

Eve, 62

Existentialism, 55, 68, 71, 122, 130

Exterior/external self, 3, 46-48, 50, 52-53, 87, 98, 113, 122-125, 133, 148

Faith, 21, 44, 49, 65, 72, 79, 137

False self, 3, 12-13, 15-16, 27, 29, 32, 37, 40, 43, 47, 69, 71, 73, 87, 98, 105, 108-109, 118, 121-126, 131-133, 148

Fénelon, François, 48

"Final Integration: Toward a Monastic Therapy," 102

Fox, Dom James, 35

Frankl, Viktor, 103

Freedom, 12, 22, 25, 30, 38, 47, 78, 92, 104-105, 114, 118, 127, 143. *See also* Liberty of spirit

Freud, Sigmund, 47, 56, 99, 128

Fromm, Erich, 103

Furlong, Monica, 9

Gandhi, 55

Genesis, 45, 61

Gethsemani, 10, 17, 20-21, 24, 26, 35, 56, 75, 97, 99

Gospel, 11, 92, 144

Grace, 7, 14-15, 17, 25, 26, 32, 60, 80, 87, 89, 101, 110, 112-115, 117-118, 122, 126, 129-130, 132

Gregory of Nyssa, 45

Hagia Sophia, 58–59, 134
Heidegger, Martin, 55, 108, 117, 138
Hinduism, 76, 79, 107, 136
Horney, Karen, 56
Humility, 16, 18–19, 23, 37, 39, 60, 65–66, 79, 84, 93, 101, 105, 133, 142–143

Identity, 12, 16, 22–23, 26, 53, 68, 71, 78, 82–86, 99, 101, 104, 113, 115, 127, 130, 133, 137, 138
"The Identity Crisis," 98
Illusory self, 5, 11, 64, 68, 71, 87, 116, 126
Image and likeness of God, 38–39, 83, 116, 131–133
Imagination, 6
Incarnation, 32, 61, 101, 111, 129, 132, 140, 143–144
Individual/individuality, 28–29, 32, 87, 90, 116, 123–125, 133
Individualism, 2, 4, 119, 123, 129
"The Inner Experience," 8, 34, 40–53, 109, 115, 133
Inner self, 3, 41–53, 73, 88, 112, 122–123, 127, 133–134, 141
Isaac of Stella, 118
Islam, 5, 7, 76, 79, 107
"Is the Contemplative Life Finished?" 137

Jesus as Mother, 58
John of the Cross, 11, 19, 23, 24, 26, 36, 44–45, 96, 111, 144
Jung, Carl, 51, 72, 99, 106, 128

Kenosis, 79, 86, 88
Kierkegaard, Soren, 99, 108, 138

"Letter to an Innocent Bystander," 56
Liberty of spirit, 39–40, 84, 105, 109, 127, 129, 136, 143. *See also* Freedom
Liturgy, 103, 107, 119, 142
Love, 2, 16, 20, 22, 25, 28, 37, 47, 59, 85, 87, 92, 110, 115, 124, 129, 132, 135, 143

Mahabalipuram, 128
The Man in the Sycamore Tree (Rice), 10
Malits, Elena, 144
Marcel, Gabriel, 63, 119
Maritain, Jacques, 18, 27–32, 48, 62, 70, 87, 91, 122, 123, 125, 133, 134, 144
Marxism and Monastic Perspectives," 97
Mary, Blessed Virgin, 58, 77
Materialism, 6, 143
Matter, 28, 61, 87, 133, 144
Medieval theology, 17
Merton, Owen, 18
Merton Studies Center, vii
Metaphysical self, 88
Middle Ages, 89, 96
Monastic fathers, 4, 26, 35, 39, 53–54, 94, 96, 108, 112, 121, 131
Monasticism, 10, 36, 54, 77–78, 84–85, 95–110, 124–125, 129, 132–134, 137, 139, 141–143, 147
Mott, Michael, 9, 35, 55, 58, 59
Mt. Athos, 108
Mozart, W. A., 69, 70
Mystical Body of Christ, 21, 33, 47, 120, 132
Mysticism, 5–6, 19, 26, 35–36, 41–42, 52–53, 79, 80, 85–86,

Mysticism (*cont'd.*), 89–91, 93, 96, 107, 118, 121–122, 124–126, 129, 131, 136, 138–139, 141, 144, 147

Narcissism, 2, 85, 86, 104, 109, 119, 124–125
Natural self, 87, 88, 99
Nature, 60, 85, 101, 102, 134
Nature/supernature, 11, 36, 59–60, 66, 71, 80, 88, 101, 131–132, 144
Neurotic self, 87, 124–125, 148
New Seeds of Contemplation, 8, 27–33
Night of the senses, 23. *See also* Dark night
Nirvana, 80, 88, 125
Nothingness, 84, 91, 111, 113–118

Obedience, 37, 38, 39, 64, 101, 133, 142, 145
Original Sin, 12, 13, 38, 39, 45, 52, 87, 115–117, 121, 133; Adam's fall, 45, 49, 53

Pascal, Blaise, 28
Pasternak, Boris, 61–62, 134
Patristic theology, 16–17
Paul, 16, 49, 63, 82, 83
Peace, 73, 75, 104, 147
Person, 32, 86–89, 91, 101, 123–124, 129, 132–133, 140
Personalism, 123, 133
Philokalia, 108
Philosophy, 96
Pius XII, 21
Polonnaruwa, 97, 127, 128
Poverty, 6, 77, 84, 105, 133
Prajna, 81, 83, 85

Prayer, 2, 6, 11, 20, 23–25, 36, 41, 77–78, 104, 107–120, 121–126, 129, 132, 139, 142, 144
Process thought, 14
Protestant theology, 55, 69
Proverbs, Book of, 58
Providence, 66
Psalms, 77, 108
Psychology, 55–56, 64, 68, 71, 79, 87, 102, 116, 122
Purity of heart, 36–38, 41, 51–52, 83, 108, 112, 133

Racism, 6, 73, 135
Rahner, Karl, 91, 145
Real self, 5, 7, 11–13, 69, 121, 126, 137
Redemption, 15, 48, 77, 101
Resurrection, 93, 139, 140
Revelation, 62
Rice, Edward, 9, 10, 34, 35, 55, 75
Robinson, J. A. T., 55
Rule of St. Benedict, 11, 21, 35, 59, 60
Russia, 62, 107

Sacrament, sacramentality, 11, 17, 60, 87, 116, 126, 143, 144
Sartre, Jean Paul, 55, 77, 99, 108, 113, 138
Satori, Zen realization, 43, 125
Scholastic tradition, 18
Second Vatican Council, 54, 73, 96, 98, 136
Seeds of Contemplation, 8, 10–27, 32, 33, 42–43, 101, 123, 131
The Seven Storey Mountain, 10, 12–13, 17, 21–22, 26, 34–35
Shakers, 107
The Sign of Jonas, 22, 62

The Silent Life, 8, 34, 35–40, 51, 53, 78, 93, 132

Sin, 8, 13, 15, 17, 32, 69, 77, 115, 117, 118, 129, 130, 134, 139

Sinai, 108

Social/political concerns, 2–3, 22, 53, 61, 104, 114, 120, 135, 141–142, 145

Solitude, 20, 22–24, 46–47, 57, 59, 71, 77–78, 97, 106, 141–142

Sophia, 59, 62, 85. *See also* Wisdom

Soul, 28

Sufism, 56, 85, 102, 103, 105, 106, 107, 145

Suicide, 64, 66

Suzuki, D. T., 42, 43, 77, 81, 83

Taoism, 105, 107

Tauler, John, 44, 45, 48, 90, 96

Teilhard de Chardin, Pierre, 55

Theological virtues, 14

Theology, 3–7, 14, 35, 78–80, 89, 93, 96, 108, 110, 116, 132, 140–141, 143, 146

Trappist, 10, 17. *See also* Cistercian

True self, 3–4, 9, 11–13, 15, 19, 20, 27, 29–33, 37–40, 51–52, 55, 68, 71, 73, 83, 92, 98, 105, 108, 114, 115, 121, 123, 125, 132–133, 139, 142–143

United States Catholic Bishops, 1, 73

Unity, 84, 114

Via negativa. See Anatta

Viet Nam War, 104

Violence, 6, 75, 77, 104, 135

Waters of Siloe, 10, 15

Wisdom, 58, 61–62, 69–74, 78–79, 82, 85, 89, 93–94, 122, 127, 131, 134–137, 140–141, 145, 147. *See also Sophia*

Withdrawal, 16–17, 27, 132, 134, 137–138, 142

Women, 58–59, 77, 134

World, 8, 73, 107, 109, 114, 120, 123, 128, 132, 142–143, 145

Zen, 42, 44, 53, 70, 75, 77–88, 92–94, 102–103, 105, 107, 110, 118, 122, 125, 126, 130, 133–136, 145, 147

Zen and the Birds of Appetite, 8, 79–94, 135, 147